English Elements
Refresher A2

Teacher's Notes

including a wide range of extra activities,
photocopiable material and
ideas for pair-finding

Sue Morris

Volkshochschule "Ehm Welk"
der Landeshauptstadt Schwerin
FB Sprachen
Puschkinstraße 13
19055 SCHWERIN
Telefon: (0385) 591 27 16

Max Hueber Verlag

Das Werk und seine Teile sind urheberrechtlich geschützt.
Jede Verwertung in anderen als den gesetzlich zugelassenen
Fällen bedarf deshalb der vorherigen schriftlichen
Einwilligung des Verlages.

Hinweis zu § 52a UrhG: Weder das Werk noch seine Teile dürfen ohne
eine solche Einwilligung überspielt, gespeichert und in ein Netzwerk
eingespielt werden. Dies gilt auch für Intranets von Firmen und von
Schulen und sonstigen Bildungseinrichtungen.

3.   2.   1. | Die letzten Ziffern
2009 08 07 06 05 | bezeichnen Zahl und Jahr des Druckes.
Alle Drucke dieser Auflage können, da unverändert,
nebeneinander benutzt werden.
1. Auflage
© 2005 Max Hueber Verlag, 85737 Ismaning, Deutschland
Redaktion: Rebecka Howe, München
Satz: Petra Obermeier, München
Herstellung: Doris Hagen
Druck und Bindung: Memminger Medien Centrum, Memmingen
Printed in Germany
ISBN 3-19-012732-8

Contents

	page
Introduction	4
Unit 1	7
Unit 2	16
Unit 3	28
Unit 4	36
Unit 5	48
Unit 6	57
Unit 7	68
Unit 8	78
Unit 9	88
Unit 10	99
Reading for fun	106

Introduction

English Elements – Refresher A2 is meant for students who have had some exposure to English, albeit not in very much depth and possibly a long time ago. They wish to reactivate their basic knowledge over a relatively short period of time.

The writers of *English Elements – Refresher A2* believe that a well-conducted English lesson should form a well-balanced whole. For this reason there is a logical progression in the activities in each unit. To help you distinguish this logical progression and to help you get the most out of the book for you and your students these *Teacher's Notes* have been written. They are thorough and, if you are an experienced teacher, you will, no doubt, ignore some of them. We hope, however, they will help you to become confident when working with the material presented in the student's book.

The notes to each separate unit of the student's book contain:
- an overview of the contents of each unit.
- step-by-step guidelines as to how to present the material in each unit.
- background information on aspects of the teaching material as appropriate.
- the tapescripts of each listening activity.
- the key to make life easier for you as a teacher.

The notes also contain:
- a section of short reading texts that help learners discover something about the UK or USA.
- a selection of extra photocopiable materials.

The Philosophy of the Student's Book

The philosophy of the *English Elements* series is that an optimum learning environment is one in which students are involved in their own learning process. To achieve such an environment a number of factors, both pedagogical and personal, need to be taken into account. Feeling comfortable with your fellow learners and seeing the relevance of your learning are two such factors that are very important. The activities in the book have been designed so that a degree of personalisation is easy to incorporate into the lessons. Fresh, modern topics have been chosen so that learners are encouraged to talk about what interests them and in so doing to improve their language skills, making them better listeners, better readers, better able to cope with real-life situations in English.

Vocabulary

There are about 1000 words in the vocabulary list at the back of the book. However, a distinction should be made between active and passive vocabulary. In the learning of vocabulary not all these words will be of interest to all students and this is where the element of choice comes in. In keeping with the learner-centred philosophy of the *English Elements* series, learners are encouraged to keep their own personal **word bank** in which they record the lexical items that they want to remember. In the **back-up sections** of each unit there are suggestions for vocabulary games that can be incorporated into classroom procedures and that will give the learners the much-needed practice in learning vocabulary.

Grammar

Although the *Refresher A2* is a book for people with some previous experience of learning English, this may be limited and have taken place a long time ago. The grammatical progression in the first four units is, therefore, a gentle one so that learners can gain confidence. The grammar is embedded in practical contexts and is kept simple. The aim of the materials is to encourage students to speak using grammar, not to learn grammar and then to speak. Students are given a reason to speak and then their attention is drawn to the grammar – the patterns they need to understand to be able to express personal meaning accurately. The grammar covered in each unit is highlighted in the coloured **grammar sections** and work is consolidated in the **grammar reference section** from pages 119-133 in the book.

The **can-do-statements** as developed and defined by the Council of Europe have been taken into consideration when writing the *Refresher A2* (for further reference see 'The European Language Certificates – Certificate in English: Learning Objectives and Test Format', published by WBT, Weiterbildungs-Testsysteme, Frankfurt).

Listening

If students are not to complain that "they talk too fast", they need to be trained in the skill of listening. Students need to be encouraged to live with uncertainty, to listen for important words in a sentence and to ignore the unimportant ones, to focus on what they *do* understand rather than what they don't. Listening texts in the book range from short, simple dialogues to telephone messages, songs and longer radio interviews. A variety of English accents are used in the listening texts.

Pronunciation

Professor Jenkins of London University has postulated that we should not expect our learners to mimic native British speakers, but that we should concentrate only on those pronunciation mistakes that hinder mutual intelligibility.
In this book we have taken a rather less radical view. Work on phonemes has been restricted to those that would cause misunderstanding if wrongly used (e.g. 'Are the fans **ch**eering or **j**eering?') but also those that might cause amusement if confused (e.g. 'I went to Holy Mess on Sunday.') Good pronunciation is not just a question of mimicking the correct sound. The use of correct word stress and getting the rhythm of a sentence right are also important aspects. There are exercises to deal with these aspects of pronunciation. It is a matter of choice whether our learners practise so that they improve in these areas.

Reading

As with listening skills, reading skills need to be developed over time. Students need to have practice in guessing unknown words, in predicting content from words or from pictures or from the title of a reading text, in extracting the relevant information from a reading text. This they will do if they have reason to read. Pair and group work activities help this reason to be more like one in real life. Texts vary from newspaper and magazine articles to an e-mail, text messages, chatroom postings, a menu and online reading material.

Writing

Writing in the main units consists of gap-filling, writing short texts or completing forms.
Practice in the skill of writing, as well as other skills needed for the examination, is given in the revision units.

Learning tips

Throughout the book there are various **learning tips** which can help students continue their learning outside the classroom. Encouraging learners to do so is important for various reasons. Firstly, the more practice the learners have in using the language the better. Secondly, time outside the classroom well used can compensate for difficulties inside it. Few groups are completely homogeneous and needs of individuals will vary. Work outside the classroom can give the weaker students time to consolidate their knowledge and it can enable the stronger students to pursue their own interests at their own pace.

Culture corner

The make-up of lower level English classes is changing and course participants often come from many different countries. Questions posed in the small **culture corner section** of each unit encourage them to share their differing experiences and so enrich the classroom experience. It must be remembered, however, that 'Sharing should be a desire and not a duty' (Bonny Tsai). No-one should be forced to talk about their own culture if they do not wish to do so.

Job talk

Students learn English for a variety of reasons. Some people may be learning English just for fun, others may want English so that they can talk to people they meet on holiday, others may need English at work. The **job talk section** of each unit deals with functional language – apologising, suggesting, asking for information – that is needed in a business situation but that can also be of interest to all participants.

Back-up section

This section is intended to give students the opportunity to do some written consolidation of material covered in class time. In this section of each unit there is a vocabulary task. Particularly in the early stages of a course such tasks can usefully be done in class time as it establishes the routine of looking back in the unit for words. It also gives you as a teacher the opportunity to reinforce the idea of the word bank. Students should be encouraged to record words that they are interested in learning. In the teacher's notes for each unit there are direct references made to exercises in the back-up section that can usefully support work done in class time. The amount of work you do in class time or leave for the students to do on their own at home will depend entirely on the make-up of your group, the motivation of your students and the time pressure under which you are working.

Can-do-statements

At the end of each back-up section you will find the can-do-statements. Students can thus see what they are learning and that can be very motivating. These statements form the basis of the syllabus for *English Elements – Refresher A2*. Self-evaluation is important here. If students feel that they are not yet confident at the skills and functions mentioned, then they should look again at the back-up section and you could refer them to a grammar book or a web-site.

Here are some which were current in February 2005 and which the authors have found helpful for students:

- **http://www.aitech.ac.jp/~iteslj/quizzes/grammar.html** or
  http://a4esl.org/q/h/grammar.html
  Exercises are grouped according to level.

- **www.englishplus.com/grammar/index.htm**
  Entries are grouped according to areas that can cause confusion. Students have to know what they're looking for and click on that 'problem' area. For example 'a' or 'an'? 'Do' or 'does'?

- **http://www.englishclub.com**
  This site has sections for grammar, listening and reading.

- **www.eslbears.homestead.com/Basic.html**
  This site has some very easy listening activities: listening for names, numbers, prices, dates, greetings and introductions, telling the time, that can give confidence to learners who don't have much opportunity to hear *simple* English spoken outside the classroom.

Revision units

Material covered in the **revision units** is designed to review work from previous units and to give practice in examination type exercises. Students are given reading, listening and speaking tasks similar to those they might face if they take the Certificate A2 examination. For example: multiple choice, true/false, reaching a consensus. There are three such units. One of two pages after unit 3, one of four pages after unit 7 and one of two pages after unit 10. Material in the revision units can, of course, be done when you wish to do so.

Time considerations

The number of lessons needed to complete *English Elements – Refresher A2* is approximately 28 double lessons of 90 minutes each. This will, of course, depend on the group you are teaching, their previous exposure to English, and how much of the back-up material you decide to integrate into classroom work. Some units have work for two double lessons, but you will probably want to spend three on others, particularly at the early stages when you are getting to know the strengths and weaknesses of your students.

The following are examples of courses and time models that could be offered:

- one semester of 14 weeks
  2 double lessons per week

- two semesters of 14 weeks
  1 double lesson per week

English Elements – Refresher A2 is intended as a framework and not a straightjacket. It should be seen as a flexible tool, a resource, a support that can help your learners achieve their goals. The essential element in encouraging learning in the classroom has always been you the teacher. We wish you luck and hope you enjoy teaching with *English Elements – Refresher A2*.

Your English Elements team

UNIT 1 About you and me

Topics:	In this unit students are encouraged to get to know each other, to tell something about themselves and their families.
Vocabulary:	names of countries; names for family relationships
Structures:	verb 'to be'; 'have got' / 'haven't got'; questions with 'Are you …?' and 'Have you got?'; plurals, apostrophe 's, personal pronouns
Functions:	introducing yourself and others; spelling names
Skills:	listening for detail (names in a family tree); reading for detail (families in different countries)
Culture corner:	family names in other countries
Learning tip:	learning vocabulary and word wheels
Reading for fun:	Text 1: Surnames
Time considerations:	As this is the first unit, timings are difficult to define precisely. You may not be able to work as fast with a new group as with one you have worked with for some time. You may have your own favourite way of starting a course. So the following is a suggestion only. lesson one: warmer, 1 and 2 lesson two: 3, 4, 5 lesson three: feedback on 'Are you …?' and 'Have you got?' from the back-up section 3; from the main unit 6 and 7

Warmer

Preparation
Get a list of participants for your new course and write the first names of everyone on adhesive labels.

In the class
Put your label on, point to it and say 'Hello, my name's …'.
Then ask students in turn 'Is your name …?' and elicit the response 'Yes, it is.' or 'No, it isn't.' Write this on the board if necessary, so that students have a model to work from.
When someone answers 'Yes, it is.' give that person the label and say 'Hello, … Nice to meet you.' and shake hands.

1 Names

Aims
– to establish the distinction between first name and surname or family name
– to introduce the alphabet and how to spell names

a Repeat your first name to the class but adding your surname. As you do so write them on the board and say 'first name' / 'surname'.

Ask for the first and surnames of the people pictured. From left to right: the actress Nicole Kidman; the actor Paul Hogan of Crocodile Dundee fame; Cathy Freeman, an athlete and winner of the 400 metres gold medal at the Sydney Olympics and the person who lit the Olympic flame in the stadium as a gesture of reconciliation between the white Australians and the Aboriginal people; the actor and film director Mel Gibson.

b Before students can do the tasks **1b/c** they will need to have some practice at spelling. Look at the **photocopiable worksheet on page 14**. Copy it onto a transparency and display it. Point to letters at random and ask students to repeat the letter chorally.

Pay particular attention to the letters that may cause problems.
German learners can confuse: a and r, e and i, g and j.

UNIT 1   7

v and w can cause problems to German, Russian and Turkish learners.

p and b can cause Russian and Arabic speakers problems.

Japanese learners will not be able to make the distinction between l and r.

A very good source of information on such problems is: Learner English, A Teacher's Guide to Interference and other Problems, 2nd edition, edited by Michael Swan and Bernard Smith (published by Cambridge University Press, 2001).

Then drill individuals. It is important not to forget this stage as it is easy for problems to remain unnoticed when all students are talking together.

Then do the listening activity. Play one short text at a time. Pause if you think it is necessary after the name has been spelled in each case so that students have time to write it down in the appropriate place. Check the answers. Ask *students* to provide the answers so that you can get a better understanding as to who is having problems.

Tapescripts 1b / Track 1

1. ▲ Think of a person.
   ● OK.
   ▲ He or she?
   ● He.
   ▲ Can you spell his surname?
   ● Right. It's G-I-B-S-O-N.
   ▲ I know. It's Mel Gibson.
   ● Yeah. That's right.

2. ▲ Think of a person
   ● OK.
   ▲ He or she?
   ● He.
   ▲ Can you spell his first name?
   ● Sure. It's P-A-U-L.
   ▲ I know. Paul McCartney.
   ● No. Try again.
   ▲ Paul Newman.
   ● No.
   ▲ Help! Can you spell his surname?
   ● H-O-G-A-N.
   ▲ Got it. Paul Hogan.
   ● Yeah. That's right.

3. ▲ Think of a person.
   ● OK.
   ▲ He or she?
   ● She.
   ▲ Can you spell her first name?
   ● Sure. It's N-I-C-O-L-E.
   ▲ I know. It's Nicole Kidman.
   ● That's right.

Key 1b

1. Mel Gibson
2. Paul McCartney, Paul Newman, Paul Hogan
3. Nicole Kidman

c Aims
 – to give practice in spelling
 – to allow students to share their knowledge of the world

Spell the name of a famous person yourself, as in the dialogues and ask the students to guess who it is, so that they understand what to do. It is important that learners are allowed to think of a famous person *they* know as it cannot be assumed that what is a household word to one student is as familiar to another.

2 Nice to meet you

Aims
 – to get the students up and moving so that they get to know more people in the class and not just the person sitting next to them
 – to consolidate work on spelling

a The name Ludmilla Taguieva has been chosen deliberately in this activitiy as if she were called Ulla Schmidt, for example, there would be no real need for a German at least, to ask her to spell it. Besides, this recognises that more and more classes are composed of students from many different countries and not just ones from Germany.

Make it clear that this dialogue is an introduction. Students have already heard you saying 'Nice to meet you' so they should passively understand this greeting. Maybe have a picture of two people shaking hands (from Clipart, for example).
Allow students to fill in the missing words in pairs and then check.

Tapescripts 2 / Track 2

Robert: Hello, my name's Robert. Nice to meet you.
Ludmilla: Nice to meet you, too. My name's Ludmilla.
Robert: And what's your surname?
Ludmilla: Taguieva.
Robert: Can you spell that, please, Ludmilla?
Ludmilla: Sure. It's T-A-G-U-I-E-V-A.
Robert: Thanks.
Ludmilla: You're welcome.

Key 2a

Robert	Ludmilla
meet	Nice
surname	Sure
spell	welcome

b Now ask students to introduce each other.

c Look at the class profile on page 17 in the student's book.

Aims
– to give students practice in spelling, a skill they will need on the phone or when checking into a hotel
– to enable students to go away from the first lesson knowing everyone's name

Allow enough time for everyone to fill in the chart.

When this activity is finished students sit down. Ask some questions to reinforce the questions with the possessive pronouns 'my/your/her/his', e.g. 'What's his first name?', 'What's her surname?', 'What's my surname?', 'What's your first name?'
If there are two people with the same first name on your group, you can also ask 'What are their names?'

If not, try to find some pictures of famous people with the same first name:
Paul Hogan, Paul McCartney, Paul Newman
David Beckham, David Bowie
Michael Schumacher, Michael Douglas
George W. Bush, George Clooney

3 Where are you from?

Aims
– to give students practice in the verb 'to be' using the question and answer 'Where are you from?' and 'I'm from …'
– to make sure all students know the English for the country where they were born
– to draw attention to the formation of plural nouns

a Check the answers. You could ask the students to spell the countries as they give you the answers so that you reinforce spelling. Make sure that the pronunciation is correct, both in terms of sounds and stress. You can make the correct stress clear in the following way:

Japan

Once you have established this system of marking stress you can use it when new words are introduced.
At this point ask if there are students in the class from countries that are not mentioned in the list and write the names of them on the board, spelling them as you do so.

Key 3a

Austria
Russia
Hungary
Switzerland
Italy
Czech Republic
Croatia
Spain
Persia (Iran)
Japan
Romania

b For this activity you will need a ball that doesn't bounce.

Ask students to stand in a circle. You start: 'I'm from ... Where are you from?' Speak slowly but naturally using the short form 'I'm ...' rather than the long form 'I am ...'. Make the melody of the question clear with a downward hand gesture.

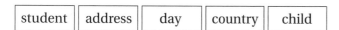

Where are you from?

Then throw the ball to another student.
Prompt, if necessary: 'I'm ... Where ...?' and gesture that they should throw the ball to another student. Continue in this way, students throwing the ball to other students until everyone has heard all the names twice. Then ask students to sit down and complete the information on page 10 in the student's book.

Then draw the students' attention to the formation of plural nouns.
Write the following words in five columns on the board:

student	address	day	country	child

Give the plural for 'student' and then ask if students can give you the others.
Establish the rule and then call out some words and ask students to decide where they go in the table. Write them up. You can do this or you can ask a student to do it for you.

Suggestions: dictionary, diary, box, watch, woman, man, person, city, journey, day, teacher, father.
This is useful for you as a teacher as you can find out how much vocabulary the students in the class already know.

Refer students to the **back-up** exercise on page 14 and the **grammar reference section** on page 120.

Extra activity
If you wish to do more work with plurals look at the **photocopiable game on page 15**.

Snap
A card game played in groups of three.
Preparation: Copy the worksheet twice per group of three and cut up the individual words and put them into envelopes. Put students into groups.

How to play: Give each group a set of these words. Ask students to shuffle the cards, deal to all players in the group, who *don't* look at them. Then have the students stand round one table and *demonstrate* the game. The first player puts a card face up on the table. Then the next player places a card on top of the first card and the third player places a card on top of that one and so on. If the word on the top card is the same as the one underneath, the first player to shout SNAP takes all the words from the pile of cards. This student has to say 'two ...' and give the correct plural of the word on the card on top. Then the game continues. The game is finished when one person has no cards left. The winner is the person with the most cards.

4 I'm or I've got?

Aims
- to introduce the verb 'have got' for possession
- to give practice using 'I am' and 'I've got'
- to introduce the idea of collocation, words that go together
- to increase students' vocabulary
- to encourage them to actively use this vocabulary to talk about themselves

a You may need to check which words are known from this list. Elicit the information as far as possible.

If you are married, point to your ring and say 'I'm married'. Take off the ring (not all the way if you are superstitious) and say 'I'm not married.' or 'I'm divorced.'
More explanations:
over 20 = 21 plus
under 40 = 39
a member of = you pay to go to the club, you are a member of the club
a commuter = I live in Darmstadt and I work in Frankfurt. I am a commuter.

Allow the students to work in pairs to complete the word wheels. Check they have made the right decisions. If many of the students have confused the two structures, then clarify the difference.

Make it clear that 'have got' is used for possession. Give an example of what you have got (e.g. 'I've got a dog, a car and a PC.').

Key 4a

I've got: a partner, a son, a bicycle, three children, a dog, a cat, a car, an e-mail address, a daughter.

I am (I'm): married, single, divorced, a member of a fitness club, over 20, interested in football, under 40, from Germany, a commuter, retired.

b Then give students one minute to look at both word wheels, ask them to close their books and then call out the words from the box on page 10 in the student's book. They have to decide if the words will go with 'I'm …' or 'I've got …'.
With a good group you could add an extra competitive element here and ask students to work in small groups and see how many extra words they can add to the word wheels. Give a time limit. The group with the most correct suggestions wins. This gives you the chance to see what information the students in your new class already know. This has the added advantage of establishing that words don't have to come *just* from the teacher. Students should be encouraged to share what they know. Draw attention to the **learning tip** and the use of word wheels. There is no *one* correct way of learning vocabulary as learning styles vary, but this idea of word wheels may be completely new to some students. They can try it for themselves and either adopt it or reject it.

c–e Demonstrate what the students have to do by writing one sentence on the board and circling the words in a sentence that are true for you. Now students read the sentences and circle the information that is true for them. In some cases they can add some information about themselves:

I'm a member of a … club.
I'm interested in …
I'm from …

Demonstrate the next phase of the task. Make it clear that it is not necessary to write whole sentences in the partner column, one word answers will do. Allow students to give each other the information.

Now draw students' attention to the grammar box at the bottom of the page. The sentences in **4c** are all with 'I've got …' or 'I am …'. What do you say for 'he' or 'she'?

Then do **4e**. Students should use the third person singular form here. 'He's/she's …' and 'He's/she's got …'.

Draw attention to exercises **2** and **3** on pages 14 and 15 in the **back-up section**. These can usefully serve as warmers at the beginning of the next lesson.

5 My family

Aims
– to introduce the words for family relationships
– to review possessive pronouns 'my' and 'your'
– to allow students to tell something about their family
– to differentiate between the 's as possession and as the short form of 'is'

a First ask the students if they know any English names. Are the names British, American or Australian? Ask students to close their eyes and just listen for names.
Write them on the board.
Then ask students to look at the family tree on page 12 and point out that they are going to hear Jennifer talking. Make sure they can see where Jennifer is in the family tree. Look at the box for Jennifer's husband. Ask 'This person is her …?' Do the same for father, brother, grandmother and children.

Then play the CD again and allow the students to fill in the names.
Allow students to check with the person sitting next to them.

Tapescript 5 / Track 3

Sandy: Have you got any pictures of your family, Jennifer?
Jennifer: I keep all my family photos in this album. Let's have a look. Look, this is Alan. It's an old picture. He was 29 then and now he's over 50! He's my husband.

UNIT 1 11

Sandy:	Who's this?
Jennifer:	This is Angela. She's my daughter. And this is Melanie. She's my second daughter.
Sandy:	Have you got a son, too?
Jennifer:	Yes, I have. One. Here's a picture of him. His name's Philip.
Sandy:	And who's this?
Jennifer:	Joe. He's my Dad and this is my mum Joan.
Sandy:	My mum's name's Joan, too.
Jennifer:	Really!
Sandy:	Yeah. It was a popular name in the late 1920's!
Jennifer:	Yeah.
Sandy:	Have you got any brothers and sisters?
Jennifer:	I haven't got any sisters, but I've got a brother. His name's Peter. Peter's married and his wife's name's Sarah.
Sandy:	This is an old photo.
Jennifer:	Yes, that's a picture of my grandparents on their wedding day in 1923. Their names were Violet and Richard. They were mum's parents.

Key 5a

From the top of the tree left to right:
Violet and Richard
Joe and Joan
Alan and Jennifer / Peter and Sarah
Angela and Melanie and Philip

b Now write two names of your family on the board. Give information about one of these people, for example 'Robert is my brother.'
Then put a question mark next to the other name. Try to elicit the question 'Who is ...?'

Then ask the students to do the task in **5b**.

Now put your family tree on the board (or bring pictures), but just write the relationships and not the names.

For example:

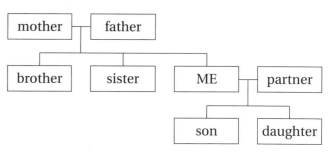

Then give information about one person, for example 'My mother's name's Janet.'
Continue with all the people. Then ask students 'What's your mother's name?' or 'What's your father's name?'
Don't insist that they use the **'s** structure here. It is, in fact, more natural to answer these questions simply with a name.
In the next part of the lesson you can encourage students to use the 's by asking 'Tell me about Robert's family.' or 'Tell me about Barbara's family.'

Refer the students to the exercises **4** and **5** in **back-up section** on pages 15-16.

6 First name or family name?

Aims
– to give students practice in reading for information
– to stimulate interest in people from other cultures where the use of names may be different
– to review passively the verbs 'have got' and 'to be'

Establish what 'true' and 'false' mean and then ask students to do the reading. You can either ask the students to read both texts or you can begin with one and the stronger students who finish quickly can go on to read the second one.
You may need to pre-teach the word 'eldest' in the first text and 'in the country' and 'forbidden' in the second. Students might be able to guess what 'forbidden' means.

Ask students to share ideas as to customs for names in other countries.
On **page 107** of the **Reading for fun section** there is a text about surnames. The aim of this section is to allow students to read more extensively.

Key 6

The Chinese family
1. false (husband)
2. true
3. false (mother and father)
4. false (Lee See Chai's grandmother)
5. true

The Malaysian family
1. false (first name)
2. true
3. true
4. false (two brothers and one sister)
5. false (she's got a cat)

Back-up section

As this is the first unit of the book it would be sensible to look at the **can-do-statements** on page 16 with your students. Then in subsequent lessons learners can look at these for themselves. These statements give learners a better understanding of what they are learning and hopefully a sense of progress.

Reference to revision unit

If your students need more practice using family words look at the revision unit on page 37.

7 Look back at the unit

Aims
– to consolidate instructions given in the first unit
– to build up vocabulary for instructions so that the classroom language can be English

Give an example as in the book to make it clear that the words are correctly written but they are in the wrong order.

the listen dialogues to → Listen to the dialogues.

Key 7

1. Write down the names that you hear.
2. Fill in the missing information.
3. Work with a partner.
4. Ask your teacher.
5. Tell your partner.
6. Look in the Back-up section.
7. Sort them out.
8. Show the names to your partner.
9. Tell the group three things about your partner.
10. Choose the words that are true for you.
11. Stand in a circle.
12. Your teacher will begin.

Photocopiable worksheet for unit 1, 1b/c: the alphabet

A	B	C	D
E	F	G	H
I	J	K	L
M	N	O	P
Q	R	S	T
U	V	W	X
Y	Z		

Photocopiable worksheet for unit 1, 3b, extra activity: plurals

address	address	address	address
bus	bus	bus	bus
surname	surname	surname	surname
child	child	child	child
woman	woman	woman	woman
student	student	student	student
person	person	person	person
country	country	country	country
city	city	city	city
book	book	book	book
teacher	teacher	teacher	teacher

UNIT 2 In my free time

Topics:	In this unit students talk about their free time activities and learn about such activities in different parts of the world.
Vocabulary:	sports and hobbies; text messages; collocations with names for sports
Structures:	indefinite articles; present simple; 3rd person **s**; questions with 'Do you …?', 'Can you …?', 'Is it …?' and short answers
Functions:	asking for information
Skills:	listening for detail about people's hobbies; reading for detail about sports around the world
Pronunciation:	listening for strong and weak forms of 'can' and 'can't'; the phonemes [s] and [z]
Job Talk:	everyday conversations in an office
Culture corner:	games in different countries
Learning tip:	word partnerships (verb + noun)
Reading for fun:	Text 2: Soccer or football?
Time considerations:	lesson 1: 1-4 plus 5 with a good group (not the photocopiable extra activity on page 26)
	lesson 2: extra activity on page 26 as a warmer, 6 and 7 (or 6 and 9)
	lesson 3: 8 and 9 or 6, 7 and 8

At the beginning of a semester there can be late enrolments for a course. If you have new people in your class make sure that you have a quick introduction so that they at least hear the names of their fellow students. You could have a chain drill round the class: 'My name's …' and 'I'm from …'. Then this person turns to the person on his or her right and this person continues 'My name is …' and 'I'm from …'.

Or ask everyone in the class to introduce one person to the new student. 'Hello … this is … She/he is … She/he's got a …'. Then you help the newcomer to respond appropriately 'Nice to meet you. My name's …'.

1 A dangerous hobby?

Aims
- to introduce the distinction between the indefinite articles 'a' and 'an'
- to practise short questions and answers with the verb 'to be'

a Ask what participants do at the weekend, in their free time. Look at the photos. Ask students to do the first task and then check the answers. You may need to help with the definition of 'dangerous' and 'exciting'. Pictures can help here (TV magazines, women's magazines, airline magazines – always help yourself to free ones!) Clip art, for example, has fishing (boring, not exciting), motor racing (dangerous).

Key 1a

(*suggestions*)
Number 3 is an energetic hobby.
Number 1 is an expensive hobby.
Number 4 is a dangerous hobby.
Number 2 is a relaxing hobby.
Number 2 is a creative hobby.
Number 3 is an exciting hobby.

b Think of a hobby yourself and ask 'What is the hobby? Ask me some questions.'

Then draw attention to 'a' or 'an' in the questions that the students are going to ask. Allow them to think of a sport or hobby and work with a partner. Then they report back to the whole class.

Then check students have understood the 'a/an' distinction. Give each student a small circle of card about 8cm in diameter (can be bought as 'Moderationskofferzubehör' or you ask your children to help you cut out small circles of card).
Ask students to write on one side 'a' and on the other side 'an'.
Then give some examples and the students have to show you the correct side of the card (e.g. energetic hobby, expensive hobby, American sport, British sport, boring hobby, dangerous sport, relaxing hobby, winter sport, summer sport, April hobby, indoor hobby, outdoor sport).

Draw attention to exercise **1** on page 26 in the **back-up section** which has work on 'a' and 'an'.

2 Your free time

Aims
– to increase students' vocabulary
– to point out more examples of collocations, words that go together
– to encourage students to think about their own hobby rather than hobbies in the abstract

a You will need to check that the words are understood. You can decide whether to do some work before the students begin the task or whether to do it when they have made a first attempt. The best way would be to have pictures as for task 1. Point out that you could say 'I like ...' with all the sports and hobbies but there are some that can't go with 'do' or 'go' or 'go to' but only with 'like' and this is what is needed here.

Divide the board into four columns. Put one example in each column so that students can maybe establish patterns. This is not always possible, but it helps in the learning process.

Key 2a

like: could be for any of the words (**must** be for: watching TV, chatting on the Internet, reading, singing)
go: windsurfing, jogging, skating, skiing, bird-watching, hiking
go to: the cinema, art galleries
play: tennis, golf, ice hockey, the piano
do: silk painting, pottery, aerobics, Tai Chi, crossword puzzles

b Allow students to write about their own hobby. They will *speak* about hobbies a little later.

3 In winter or in summer?

Aims
– to give practice in listening for information
– to reinforce some vocabulary for sports and hobbies

a, b Before you play the CD ask students to predict some sports and hobbies they will hear. What sports are typical winter sports and which are summer sports? Where do countries have dry and wet seasons rather than summer and winter? What sports are played there?

Then play the CD and ask them to fill in the missing information. Check. Then play the CD again and allow students to answer the 'true/false' questions.

Tapescripts 3 / Track 4

1. ▲ This is Jan and he's from Australia. Tell us about your hobbies Jan. What about the summer?
   ● Your summer or my summer?! The long summer holidays are in December in Australia. In December and January I go surfing along the coast in Queensland and go diving on the barrier reef. Diving is wonderful but it's an expensive hobby. In the winter I go skiing. Of course, there isn't a lot of skiing in Australia as there is in Europe but we have snow in the

Blue Mountains north of Sydney. When I go skiing I take a lot of photographs. I do a lot of photography in the winter.

2. ▲ What are your hobbies Bob?
   ● Well, I live in Canada so in the winter I play ice hockey on the lake near my house because it's very cold and the lake is often frozen. It's a very energetic and dangerous sport. I broke my nose last winter. And in summer. Well, I also go hunting in the forest with my friend Paul and I play basketball. I play in a team but I'm not very good.

3. ▲ Hi, I'm Doug and I'm from San Diego in California.
   ● Tell us about your hobbies Doug.
   ▲ My main hobby is soccer. In Europe you call it football. OK, that's in the winter and in the summer I play baseball, a typically American sport. It's an energetic sport but it's not really dangerous and I go swimming, but not outside. There's a big indoor swimming pool near my house.

4. ▲ Shashi's from India. Tell us about your hobbies Shashi.
   ● Well, I play cricket. A lot of people think that cricket is very boring but I love it. It's a complicated sport but it isn't boring at all. We don't have winter and summer in India. We have the wet and the dry season. From June to September it can be very wet and then I don't play cricket, I like reading books then.

Key 3

Jan
In the summer he goes surfing and diving.
In the winter he goes skiing and does photography.
true, true, false (in the winter)

Bob
In the winter he plays ice hockey.
In the summer he goes hunting and plays basketball.
true, true, false (in the summer), false (a basketball team)

Doug
In the winter he plays soccer.
In the summer he plays baseball and goes swimming.
false (soccer and baseball), true

Shashi
In the dry season he plays cricket.
In the wet season he likes reading.
false (in the dry), true

C Refer back to what students wrote in **2b**. Do any of them have the same hobbies as Jan, Bob, Doug and Shashi? Draw attention to the s in the third person singular.

Draw attention to exercise **2a** on page 26 of the **back-up section** which has work on the third person singular **s**.

Note that the s can have different sounds. This is the lead-in to **4**.

4 Sounds [s] and [z]

Aims
– to give students practice in distinguishing between the sounds [s] and [z]

First make the two sounds clearly yourself. Ask students to feel the puff or air on their hands when they make the sound [s] and the vibration in their throat when they say [z]. Students then listen and tick the word they hear. Then they choose a word themselves and 'dictate' to their partner. Often students don't *hear* the difference between similar sounds in English and this helps them to develop this ability.

You could then refer back to the sports and ask students to decide if the s sounds like [s] or [z].
He does Tai Chi.
She plays basketball.
He goes skiing.
She likes watching TV.

Tapescripts 4 / Track 5

pens   [z]
bus   [s]
zoo   [z]
place [s]
said   [s]
lose   [z]
juice [s]

5 Guess the hobbies

Aims
- to introduce the question 'Do you …?' for passive understanding and active use
- to introduce the third person singular question 'Does he/does she …?' for passive understanding and active use

a You need to think carefully about task **5** on page 21 so that you know exactly who is going to work with whom. Look at the **photocopiable worksheet on page 24** to help you in setting up the task.

b Now students ask questions to find out if their guesses were right.
A talks to C and B talks to D.
Then A talks to D and B talks to C.

c Then have some feedback.

d You can approach this task in two ways.

Either:
Make 4 columns on the board. Ask students to give you the names of all the hobbies they remember from **2a** and write them in the left-hand column on the board. Then choose between two and four students as shown and write the names in columns 2, 3, and 4.
You ask the first few questions using 'Does X …?' and elicit the answer 'Yes, he does.' or 'No, he doesn't.'
Do this as often as you think is necessary and then encourage the students themselves to ask the questions. Your job is then to fill in the columns with ✓ or ✗ as appropriate.

Or:
Display an OHT of the **photocopiable worksheet on page 25** in which the hobbies have already been listed. The advantage is that this saves time, but the disadvantage is that it doesn't involve the students in thinking of sports and hobbies for themselves. Otherwise the procedure is the same. Ask random questions about two or three students and then encourage students to ask the questions.

e Personalises the grammar. Students share what they have discovered about their fellow students. They can also add information about themselves if this seems appropriate 'Thomas likes reading but he doesn't go skiing. I go skiing but I don't like reading.'

Look at the **grammar box** at the bottom of page 21 and point out the s that is used for the third person singular. Also point out that it is, however, only used once, so 'Does he go …?' *not* 'Does he goes …?'

Refer students to the **back-up section** exercise **2b** on page 26 for some work with the present simple.

Extra activity
If students need some reinforcement of the grammar before they go home to work on their own from the **back-up section** look at the **photocopiable worksheet on page 26**. If you use these materials it is a good idea to laminate them so that you can use them again and again.

Procedure:
You will need tables for this activity.

Copy one worksheet for each group of three students in your class. (If you have only four students, have two groups of two.) Cut up the words and put into envelopes.
Give an envelope to each group and give them a time limit of 5-10 minutes. Ask them to make as many sensible questions and answers as possible with the words. If groups use all their cards but can still think of more sentences, they can write them on a piece of paper. When the task is over and before oral feedback, allow groups to look at each other's efforts. It is good to allow groups to share ideas.

6 Why not?

Aims
- to introduce and practise the modal verb 'can' for ability
- to sensitise students to the way short answers reflect the questions posed 'Can you …?' ('Yes, I can.' / 'No, I can't.') and 'Do you …?' ('Yes, I do.' / 'No, I don't.')
- to have fun with text messages
- to encourage learners to bring what they know into the classroom

a In the previous lesson students have been asking and answering questions with 'Do you …?' and answering 'Yes, I do.' and 'No, I don't'. In this lesson there is a similar pattern with the question 'Can you … ?' – 'Yes, I can.' or 'No, I can't.'

First establish the idea of 'can' for ability. Write something *very very* small on the board and ask 'Can you read that?' to elicit the answer 'No, I can't.' Rub off the word(s). Write them again only fractionally bigger. Continue and write bigger until the answer to the question is 'Yes, I can.'

Point out the different sounds in the questions and in the answer. Then play the CD and ask students to decide which sounds they hear. Play the CD all the way through and then go back and stop it to check which sounds the students hear.

Tapescripts 6a / Track 6

▲ Do you like chatting on the Internet?
● No, I don't.
▲ Why not?
● Well, I can type but I can't type fast and I don't understand all text messages.
▲ Can YOU text?
● Yes, I can. It's easy!

Key 6a

1. Well, I can [kən] type but I can't [kɑːnt] type fast and I don't understand all text messages.

2. Can [kən] YOU text?
   Yes, I can [kæn]. It's easy!

b Ask the questions and then ask the students if they know what the text messages mean.

Key 6b

2nite	Tonight
HaPEBday	Happy birthday.
HaPEHolidAz	Happy holidays.
THNQ	Thank you.
URGr8	You are great.
CU	See you.
MunE$$$£££MunE	Money, money, money, money
RUOK	Are you OK?

There are some more messages on the **photocopiable worksheet on page 27**. By drawing learners' attention to English they may read in cyberspace, it makes them understand how much English they can learn outside the classroom. You can ask *them* to add to your text messages!

WLDne!	well done
URBtifl	you are beautiful
LUL	love you lots
DWBH	don't worry be happy
LkEU	lucky you
Nva2L8	never too late
THX	thanks
RLX	relax
Go4It	go for it
TakItEzE	take it easy
FYI	for your information
G2G	got to go

c First show students that they should read the activities in column one and decide if they can or can't do them. You might need to explain 'change the oil' and 'chopsticks'. They write 'Yes, I can.' or 'No, I can't.' next to each activity in column 2. Then they work with a partner and ask him or her about the activities using 'Can you ...?' and they then fill in 'Yes, he/she can.' or 'No, he/she can't.' in the third column.

d Have a feedback session.
If you have a group with students who use English for their job you could do optional task **8** at this point.

7 Games in different countries

Aims
– to bring all the grammar of the unit together
– to give students practice in reading for detail
– to encourage shyer students to talk in the unthreatening atmosphere of a small group

This is the first example in the book of the use of the **files section**. It is important if questions are to be realistic that students don't ask each other questions the answers to which they already know. To this end, in some units there are texts in the main body of a unit and some in the files section appropriate for that unit. This is such an example. The text on page 23 is slightly more difficult than the one on page 106 in the file section.

The procedure for this task is as follows.
1. Divide your class into two groups A and B. If it is larger than twelve then you will need four groups (in this case ask *two* groups to read the text on page 23 and *two* groups to read the text on page 106)
2. Ask group A to look at the text about Sepak Takraw on page 23 and group B to look at the one about Kudoda on page 106. Focus their attention on the questions. They need to find the answer to these questions in the text. Allow them to read and try to find the answers. Encourage students to work together to find the answers. Thus the weaker students can be helped by their fellow students at this stage. This is important so that they will be able to cope when they work in pairs later in the activity. Your role is to be on hand to help with vocabulary if necessary.
   The words that might pose problems:
   Sepak Takraw – team, kick, isn't exactly dangerous, hurt yourself, plastic, court, serves, set, scores
   Kudoda – bowl, stones, break, pick up
3. Give each person in the two groups (or in the four groups) a number.
4. Ask all the people with the same number to work together either as a pair or as a group of four. So the people from group A should *ask* their partner questions about Kudoda and *answer* their partner's questions about Sepak Takraw. The students from group B should *ask* their partners about Sepak Takraw and *answer* their partner's questions about Kudoda.

Key 7

Kudoda	**Sepak Takraw**
1. No, it isn't.	Yes, it is.
2. No, it isn't.	Yes, it is.
3. No, it isn't.	No, it isn't.
4. A team game but you can play alone, too.	A team game.
5. Any number.	Three.
6. No, you don't: stones/marbles and a bowl.	No, you don't. A net and a ball.
7. Outside.	Outside or inside.
8. Yes, you can. The person who picks up the most stones.	Yes, you can. The team that wins 2 sets.

C Ask students if they know of any games from a different culture. There is the danger here that students lapse into German. You could try to avoid this by giving a skeleton to talk about a game:
It is a game for … players.
You play it inside/outside.
You need … when you play it.
The person who / the team that … is the winner.

If students enjoy reading and are interested in sports, draw their attention to the **Reading for fun section** where number 2 on **page 108** is about sports: Soccer or football?

8 Office talk

This task is optional and may not be of interest to students who do not use English for their job.

Aims
– to give students practice in making small talk to visitors
– to show how the grammar of the unit can be useful in everyday situations

Brainstorm what topics are appropriate for small talk with a visitor to a company. Allow students to sort out the lines of the four small dialogues. Within each dialogue the lines are in the wrong order but they are not mixed between different dialogues.

Key 8a

1. ▲ Do you play golf?
   ● Yes, I do. My handicap is not very good, though. It's 18.
   ▲ That's no problem. Would you like to play on Saturday?
   ● That would be very nice.
   ▲ Good. See you on Saturday.
   ● Fine. I look forward to it.

2. ▲ Are you interested in ice hockey?
   ● Yes, I am. The local team in Canada is very good.
   ▲ Would you like to go to a game on Saturday? I can get tickets from a friend.
   ● I'm sorry, I can't this weekend.
   ▲ And next week?
   ● Yes, that would be fine.
   ▲ Fine. See you on Saturday then.

3. ▲ Is this your first visit to Munich?
   ● Yes, it is.
   ▲ Would you like to go on a tour of Ludwig's castles?
   ● Oh, yes. I'd like that very much.
   ▲ Good. I can book the tour for Saturday. See you then.
   ● See you then. I look forward to it.

4. ▲ Good morning. Can I help you?
   ● Good morning. I've got an appointment with Mr. Harris.
   ▲ I'm sorry, Mr Harris is still in a meeting.
   ● That's OK. I'm early.
   ▲ Do sit down. Would you like a coffee?
   ● Sorry, I don't drink coffee, but tea would be nice.
   ▲ With milk and sugar?
   ● Black with no sugar.

Allow students to practise the dialogues in pairs. Then point out the difference between 'Do you like ...?', 'Would you like ...?' and 'Would you like to ...?'
Do you like? *(every day, in general)*
Would you like + noun? *(now, on one occasion)*
Would you like to + verb?

Write 'Would you like ...?' on the board and see in how many different ways the class members can complete the sentence (e.g. a cup of tea, coffee, a drink, some water, some coffee).
('some' pre-empts unit 4, but some students may already remember this from their previous learning and this is all to the good.)

Do the same for 'Would you like to ...?'
Then draw attention as to how you can reply to these questions with an affirmative or polite 'no' answer.

Then you could use a ball that doesn't bounce and ask students to pose a question and throw the ball to another student who then has to answer it. Continue until everyone has had a turn at asking and answering a question.

c   This task focuses on a method for increasing vocabulary not as units of one word, but as chunks of language.

See you: later / on Saturday / next week / tomorrow / soon.

You can then always say 'See you next week' as you say 'goodbye' to your students and encourage them to say the same to their fellow students so that this chunk of language becomes part of their everyday vocabulary, thus increasing their fluency.

9 Everyday English

Aims
– to show how the grammar of the unit can be useful in everyday life
– to give learners practice in listening to everyday English
– to sensitise students to the melody of English

a   As you read the dialogue to your students make sure that you use the correct intonation.

Excuse me.

Or alternatively you can use cuisenaire rods (small blocks of wood used in primary Maths classrooms) and use two different sized rods of two different colours to show how the voice goes up in the middle of this phrase.

Drill the questions with different content:

Excuse me, does this bus go to Oxford Circus
Prompt: Piccadilly. – Excuse me, does this bus go to Piccadilly Circus?
Prompt: Train. – Excuse me, does this train go to Piccadilly Circus?
Prompt: Glasgow. – Excuse me, does this train go to Glasgow?
Prompt: Coach. – Excuse me, does this coach go to Glasgow?

Then allow students to do the matching activity in pairs. They check their answers and you then play the CD to check.

Tapescripts 9 / Track 7

A: Excuse me, does this train stop <u>in Birmingham</u>?
B: No, it doesn't. You want the one <u>from platform 9</u>.
A; <u>Cheers mate.</u>
B: <u>You're welcome.</u>

A: Excuse me, does this bus go to <u>Heathrow</u>?
B: Yes, it does. It goes to <u>all four London airports. Heathrow, Gatwick, Stansted and Luton.</u>
A: <u>Thanks a lot.</u>
B: <u>Not at all.</u>

A: Excuse me, does the coach to <u>Bath</u> leave from here?
B: No, it doesn't. You need <u>stop number 4</u>. Over there where there's a queue.
A: <u>Thanks.</u>
B: <u>Not at all.</u>

Key 9

1c, 2a, 3b

b Then students practise the dialogues in pairs. They can look at the **tapescript** on page 134 and change the underlined parts of the dialogue as they wish.

Note: Use of the tapescripts can be helpful, but you should discourage your students from looking at the tapescripts while they are listening if your aim in the activity is to help improve their listening comprehension.

Reference to revision unit

If your students need some more reading practice and practice at asking questions, look at revision unit 1 on page 36.

Photocopiable worksheet for unit 2, 5a

	Name of students	first partner	second partner
A	Eva Schmidt	C	D
B	Gerti Liedtke	D	C
C	Jochen Sudbrack	A	B
D	Anika Stoiber	B	A
E		G	H
F		H	G
G		E	F
H		F	E
I		K	L
J		L	K
K		I	J
L		J	I
M		O	P
N		P	O
O		M	N
P		N	M

How to use this table:

1. Copy the table.
2. Write the students' names in the correct column.
3. Then tell the students who they will be working with.
   So, for example, Eva (A) will work with Jochen (C) and Anika (D).
4. Allow students to fill in their guesses about the students they are going to work with on page 21 of the student's book. So Eva fills in her guesses about Jochen first and then those for Anika. Jochen fills in his guesses about Eva and Gerti and Anika fills in her guesses about Gerti and Eva. Gerti fills in her guesses about Anika and Jochen.

This activity is designed to allow a large class to do a lot of talking. If your group is very small or if it doesn't easily divide into smaller groups of four, ask students to simply write down some guesses for what hobbies their fellow students have.
'I think Eva likes .../ goes .../ plays ...' and then ask them in a whole class situation to ask the questions.

Photocopiable worksheet for unit 2, 5d

Hobby	Student 1	Student 2	Student 3	Student 4
skiing	✗	✓	✗	✓
windsurfing				
jogging				
skating				
bird-watching				
hiking				
cards				
tennis				
golf				
the piano				
ice hockey				
watching TV				
chatting on the Internet				
reading				
the cinema				
art galleries				
silk painting				
aerobics				
Tai Chi				
crossword puzzles				

Photocopiable worksheet for unit 2, extra activity, after 5e

Do	you	they	he	like
Does	she	go	go to	play
do	at the weekend	in the summer	in the winter	tennis
golf	ice hockey	skating	skiing	every weekend
aerobics	Tai Chi	in his	in her	free time
?	?	?	?	does
in your	in their	do	they	does
reading	bird-watching	art galleries	the cinema.	the piano
Yes,	Yes,	No,	No,	he
doesn't.	don't.	don't.	doesn't.	I

Photocopiable worksheet for unit 2, 6b

WLDne!
URBtifl
LUL
DWBH
LkEU
Nva2L8
THX
RLX
Go4It
TakItEzE
FYI
G2G

UNIT 3   On the road

Topics:	In this unit students talk about numbers of all sorts and are encouraged to ask a lot of questions.
Vocabulary:	car registration numbers; phone numbers; telling the time
Structures:	questions in present simple; question words: what, when, where, who, how; prepositions of time
Functions:	asking questions; expressing time
Skills:	listening for detail (numbers and time); selective reading (rental car details)
Job Talk:	renting a car on-line
Culture corner:	phone numbers and how to answer the phone
Learning tip:	collecting expressions with prepositions
Reading for fun:	Text number 3 on page 109 is about the traditional British milkman or milk lady who still delivers milk to the door in some areas of Britain, particularly rural ones.
Time considerations:	lesson 1: 1-3 or 4 lesson 2: (4) 5 and 6

Now that you are beginning unit three the students in your class should know each other quite well. Often the same students work together. For some classes this works well and disrupting the 'normal' seating plan can be unsettling. It is sometimes, however, a good idea to have students work with a new partner so that they hear a different voice and may benefit from a different perspective on learning. If you feel this would be a good idea you can use the following warmer for this unit.

Warmer

Copy the **photocopiable worksheet on page 34** and cut up the words. Give each student a word and they have to find their partner. The people who have got a card with 'a' or 'an' ask e.g. 'Have you got a (racing car)?' And the people asked answer 'Yes, I have.' or 'No, I haven't.' If you have an odd number in the class give two people the same card.
This reviews grammar from the first unit and the indefinite articles 'a' and 'an' and it forms a bridge to the first task in the unit.

Ask students to sit down with their partner.

1   What's his car registration number?

Aims
– to reinforce the third person singular **s**
– to introduce the theme of numbers

a   Ask students to work in pairs and complete the first task. Then check.

Key 1a

1. photo 4
2. photo 1
3. photo 3
4. photo 2

b Aim
– to practise the letters of the alphabet again.

Draw attention to the **culture corner section** at the bottom of page 28 and collect any other ideas about car registration numbers.

Background information
Car registration numbers in the UK used to comprise a letter, three numbers and three letters. The first letter told you when the car was registered and the last three letters where it was registered. New registration numbers used to be introduced every August and so you could tell immediately who had just bought a brand-new car. This system has been completely changed and new cars are registered twice a year. The change was aimed to help the demand for new cars remain steady throughout the year. In the UK it is difficult to tell where a car comes from. Letters in registration numbers don't help you! So, for example, the number VN04 XLY tells you that the car was registered in 2004 and that it was registered in the county of Gloucestershire (V!). When a car is registered in the UK it keeps its registration number until 'it dies'. It doesn't have a new registration number when the owner moves house as it is the case in Germany.

2 Numbers

Aims
– to sensitise students to numbers
– to show how various numbers are expressed in English

a Ask students to fill in the missing vowels.

Key 2a

telephone number
extension number
mobile number
identity card number
passport number
PIN (personal identification number)
credit card number

Any other suggestions:
social security number (in Britain this would be your National Health number)
house number
bank card number

b Ask students to work in pairs and to predict what the numbers will be and what 'It's a secret.' means. Then play the CD to check.

Tapescripts 2b / Track 8

▲ What's your telephone number?
● It's 0044 1729830468.

▲ What's your extension number?
● 3920.

▲ What's your credit card number?
● 3750 30123822006.

▲ What's your PIN number?
● It's a secret!

▲ What's your mobile number?
● 0177 456 4540.

Key 2b

telephone
extension
credit card
PIN
mobile

c Before students can do task **2c** you need to draw their attention to the way phone numbers are given.
0 in a phone number is pronounced 'oh' in British English and 'zero' in American English.
Write a selection of phone numbers on the board and ask students at random to say them.

Then dictate five phone numbers to the whole class. As a check ask three good students to write the answers on the board. Choose students you know will probably get it right, otherwise you are exposing students to unnecessary embarrassment. Then ask students to do the pair work **2c**.

Partner A looks in the file section on page 106 and dictates the numbers there to his or her partner who writes them in columns 1-4 in **2c** on page 29. Partner B looks in the file section on page 109 and dictates the numbers to his or her partner who writes them in columns 1-4 on page 29. Both students fill in the phone numbers in **2c** but they both write *different* numbers.

Then they should *guess* where the people come from.

Key 2c

Partner A
1. Mr Ishiguro: 0081 3529955568 — Japan
2. Ms Wallner: 0043 14567252 — Austria
3. Mr & Mrs May: 0044 1296776290 — GB
4. Mr Sigasa 0027 124216302 — South Africa

Partner B
1. Mr Kashino: 0081 744227698 — Japan
2. Ms Häberli: 0041 264675257 — Switzerland
3. Mr President 001 7032629196 — USA
4. Mr Hewitt (Leyton Hewitt is a tennis player) 0061 262451 52 — Australia

Background information: answering the phone

Italy — 'Pronto' which literally means 'I am ready.'
France — Allô.
UK — In private homes the person answering the phone doesn't usually give the name but the number: 'Oxford 65934.' So if you don't recognise who is on the phone you have to ask: 'Is that ...?' or 'Hello, this is (give your name).' And ask: 'Can I speak to ..., please?' If you want to speak to Barbara and Barbara IS on the phone, she'll say: 'Speaking.' ('Could I speak to Barbara, please?' – 'Speaking.' // This IS Barbara.)
USA — Hello.

d You will need a ball that doesn't bounce for this activity. Stand in a circle. Ask a question about numbers and throw the ball to a student who has to answer the question.
With a weak group remind the students of the possible questions with numbers from the beginning of **2** before they start.

What's your phone number?
It's ...
What's your PIN number?
It's a secret!

3 Questions and answers

Aims
– to introduce other wh-question words
– to clarify the meaning of these question words

a Before you ask students to do the task give an example. Write some answers on the right-hand side of the board.

When do you ...?   At the weekend.
                    On Saturday.
                    At the weekend.

Ask: 'What could the question be?' Then write the question on the left-hand side of the board. Then let students complete the task and check the answers.

Key 3a

1. When
2. Where
3. Who – Note: Students who learnt English a while ago might ask about the question word 'Whom?' – 'Whom did you meet ...?' is grammatically accurate, but is not used in English in everyday speech now. You would be doing your learners a disservice if you insisted on this usage as it is old-fashioned.
4. How
5. Who
6. Why
7. Where
8. Why

b Ask students to match the question words with possible answers.

Aims
– to reinforce the question words and appropriate answers
– to check understanding of the meaning of the wh-question words
– to reinforce the question form 'Do you ...?' and 'Does he/she ...?' in the present simple
– to introduce prepositions of time for passive understanding

Key 3b

When?	– at Christmas, at six o'clock, in the winter, in the summer, on my birthday
Where?	– in London, in Italy, in the city
What?	– coffee, toast, squash
Why?	– because it helps me to sleep, because it's good exercise, because it's cheap
How?	– on foot, by plane, by car, by bus
Who?	– my brother, two colleagues, my boss

The question words 'who' and 'where' are often confused by German learners. If your learners do so, refer them to exercise **1** in the **back-up section** on page 34.

Give an example of a question that could be formed with the words from **3b**, e.g. 'What does he eat for breakfast?' or 'How do you get to work?'

Focus on 'do/does' and ask when you use which? Check the **grammar box** with the structures.

c Then allow students to make up their own questions and then to stand up and ask three people in the group these questions.

Have a feedback session.

Draw students' attention to exercise **2** on page 34 in the **back-up section**.

4 Excuse me, have you got the time?

Aims
- to practise the third person singular questions with 'does'
- to introduce telling the time
- to reinforce the use of 'Excuse me, …?' in enquiries and the appropriate use of 'Thank you.' and 'You're welcome.'
- to draw attention to the [IZ] pronunciation of the third person singular present

a Match the sentences with the clock times.

Key 4a

1. photo 4
2. photo 3
3. photo 1
4. photo 2

Before students can do the listening task you will need to do some work with times. You will need a clock. If you don't have one easily available, use an overhead transparency on which you have drawn a clock and use two pencils, one longer than the other as the clock hands. Show times on the clock and say the appropriate times. Repeat so that students hear them more than once. Then show clock times and ask students to tell *you* the times.

At this point use: 'ten past ten' rather than 'ten ten', 'half past ten' rather than 'ten-thirty'. Next *write* some times on the board, for example, 4.15, 9.20, 11.40 and ask for the times as you have just drilled.

Point out that you often *write* the time with the figures but you often *say* the time with 'past' and 'to'.
10.10 = ten past ten
11.40 = twenty to twelve

Note: telling the time in American English
10.20 = twenty after ten
10.40 = twenty before eleven

b Now ask students to listen to the CD and write down in figures the times they hear. The last one is complicated and will need to be played more than once! To aid comprehension you could first ask students to listen and answer the questions: 'Where are the people?' or 'Where will the people be at 8 o'clock?' Then you can ask: 'Is it morning or evening?'

Tapescript 4b / Track 9

1. ▲ Excuse me, have you got the time?
   ● Sure. It's quarter to four.
   ▲ Thanks.

UNIT 3

2. ▲ Excuse me, have you got the time?
   ● Yeah. It's eleven thirty.
   ▲ Thanks very much.
   ● You're welcome.

3. ▲ Got the time mate?
   ● Ten to nine.
   ▲ Cheers.

4. ▲ What time do you make it?
   ● Twenty-five past.
   ▲ I think my watch is slow. I make it twenty past.
   ● Never mind. We're not late. I said we'd meet Jim and Ann in the bar at half past so we can have a drink before the concert starts at 8.

Key 4b

1. quarter to four (3.45)
2. eleven thirty (11.30)
3. ten to nine (8.50)
4. twenty-five past (7.25), twenty past (7.20), half past (7.30), eight (8.00)

Draw attention to the different ways in which you can ask for the time and which are formal and more informal.

Informal	More formal
(Have you) got the time (mate)?	Excuse me, have you got the time?
What time do you make it?	

Also note the meaning of 'My watch is slow.' and 'My watch is fast.'

If students find listening hard and want some extra practice the web-site **www.eslbears.homestead.com/Basic.html** has simple listening tasks with telling the time.

C Students work with a partner to find out about routines and times.

Aims
– to practise the times
– to reinforce the third person singular **s**

Ask students to look at the row of clocks and point out that there is one blank for them to write their own sentence. Then explain the task. First, students write the times at which they do the various things in the clocks in the top row. Then they ask their partner questions 'What time do you ...?' so that they can fill in the information about their partner on the second row.

Refer students to exercise **3** in the **back-up section** on page 34. This aims to combine the written and the spoken forms of telling the time.

Ask students to share their knowledge about different times of starting work in different countries from the **culture corner section**. You don't need to restrict the activity to times of work. You could widen it to include a discussion of times in general.

Background information
In general work starts later in Britain than in Germany. A normal working day is often said to be 9 a.m. to 5 p.m., but as with all western countries people in work seem to be working longer and longer hours. Schools normally start at 9 o'clock and finish at three or four in the afternoon with a lunch break in the middle of the day. In November 2004 Tony Blair, the British Prime Minister, announced plans to allow children to stay at school with supervision from 8 in the morning to 6 o'clock in the evening. The plan was one aimed to help working mothers. Large supermarkets open at 7.30 or 8 but high street shops usually open at 9. Food shops are opening longer now with some open until 9 or 10 in the evening and all night shopping is now a reality in some areas of Britain. Sunday shopping is also normal now and it is not only supermarkets that open their doors on this day.

Extra activity

If you want to give learners practice in using the times again, look at the **photocopiable worksheet on page 35**. There are enough for three groups of two on this worksheet, so copy it as many times as you need to. If you have a class where the number of students doesn't divide neatly into twos, have one group of three.

Then cut up the worksheet in strips. So the first strip is:

early.	The milkman gets up

Give each pair all the strips. The aim is to put the strips together to form a circle.

Players do this by playing 'dominoes'. So from the first domino you add as follows:

| until 9 o'clock. | He goes to bed | early. | The milkman gets up | at four o'clock. | He has break-fast |

They play until one pair has completed the circle. If you have the element of competition, this pair are the winners.

This task also prepares students for work on routines in the next unit.

If students enjoy reading, point out that text number 3 on **page 109** in the **Reading for fun section** is about the traditional British milkman.

5 Prepositions

Aim
– to draw attention to the use of prepositions of time

Ask students to do the task and make their own decisions as to the rules for the use of these prepositions.
Exercise **5b** could be done at home along with exercise **4** from the **back-up section**.

Key 5b

1. in
2. at, at
3. at, on
4. in, in
5. at
6. on, on
7. on, in

6 Rent a car

Aims
– to give students practice in selective reading
– to expose learners to the sort of forms that they will see when booking on-line
– to show how English can be useful outside the classroom

a First ask some questions about cars: 'Have you got a car?', 'What sort of car do you drive?', 'Has your car got air-conditioning?' or 'Has it got power-steering?'

Then ask some questions from page 32 in the student's book:

How many suitcases can you take with you in a Vauxhall Omega?
How many people can sit in a Ford Focus?
Has the Vauxhall Corsa got air-conditioning?
Is the Renault Espace an automatic car?

In this way you can check if vocabulary has been understood.

Then ask students to do the task at the top of page 33 alone and then to check with a partner.
This sort of task will come up in the A2 certificate examinations.

Key 6a

Tom and Lisa:	Renault Espace
Jana and Alex:	Vauxhall Omega
Sarah:	Peugeot 307
Ranjit and Romy:	Ford Focus

b First clarify some vocabulary: a business trip (German learners tend to say a business journey), rental, to pick up the car, following (Friday), details, requirements, postcode, mainland

Explain this is the sort of form they will see if they want to book a hotel or a rental car or pay for something from an English web-site.
Draw learners' attention to the 'Pick up/ Return lines' at the bottom of the page. They can see dates and times very faintly printed. This is to show them that they should add the date and the time when *they* want to pick up their car.

Allow students to fill in their details. Then ask a few of them what sort of car they want and ask why.

3

Back-up section

Reference has been made throughout the unit to exercises from this section that are appropriate. The vocabulary revision task for this unit is a crossword. If your learners like doing this sort of puzzle, you can make your own very quickly by visiting the web-site: www.puzzlemaker.com

Reference to revision unit

If your students need some more practice with spelling and listening to numbers, look at the listening section in the revision unit on page 37.

Photocopiable worksheet for unit 3, warmer

Fiat	an Italian car
Volvo	a Swedish car
Renault	a French car
BMW	a Bavarian car
Chrysler	an American car
Ferrari	a racing car
Seat	a Spanish car
Trabi	an old East German car
Rover	a British car
Rolls Royce	an expensive British car

© 2005 Max Hueber Verlag
This sheet may be photocopied and used within the class.

34 UNIT 3

Photocopiable worksheet for unit 3, extra activity

early.	The milkman gets up
at four o'clock.	He has breakfast
at half past four.	He leaves the house at
five o'clock.	He delivers the first pint
of milk at quarter to six.	He finishes his milk round
at half past twelve.	He drives his van back
to the dairy.	He goes home
and has lunch at 2 o'clock.	In the afternoon he
works in his garden.	In the evening he has supper
at quarter past seven.	He watches television
until 9 o'clock.	He goes to bed
early.	The milkman gets up
at four o'clock.	He has breakfast
at half past four.	He leaves the house at
five o'clock.	He delivers the first pint
of milk at quarter to six.	He finishes his milk round
at half past twelve.	He drives his van back
to the dairy.	He goes home
and has lunch at 2 o'clock.	In the afternoon he
works in his garden.	In the evening he has supper
at quarter past seven.	He watches television
until 9 o'clock.	He goes to bed
early.	The milkman gets up
at four o'clock.	He has breakfast
at half past four.	He leaves the house at
five o'clock.	He delivers the first pint
of milk at quarter to six.	He finished his milk round
at half past twelve.	He drives his van back
to the dairy.	He goes home
and has lunch at 2 o'clock.	In the afternoon he
works in his garden.	In the evening he has supper
at quarter past seven.	He watches television
until 9 o'clock.	He goes to bed

© 2005 Max Hueber Verlag
This sheet may be photocopied and used within the class.

UNIT 4 No time

Topics:	In this unit students talk about routines, stress and how to cope with it.
Vocabulary:	time expressions; everyday activities; routines
Structures:	questions with 'How often …?'; adverbs of frequency; questions with 'How much …?' and 'How many …?'; some and any
Functions:	making suggestions; accepting and rejecting suggestions
Skills:	listening for detail in a radio programme; reading for detail from a web-site
Pronunciation:	listening for the difference in the two sounds [e] and [æ]
Job Talk:	making a booking (table at a restaurant or a conference room at a hotel)
Culture corner:	how many days holidays people have in different countries
Learning tip:	listening for words in a song; listening for specific sounds
Reading for fun:	Text number 4 on page 110 is about the city of Bath, a spa in Britain where Queen Victoria went to drink the waters.
Time considerations:	lesson 1: 1–2 lesson 2: 3, 4, 5 lesson 3: 6 and 7 Optional extra 8

Warmer

Review the time: write some times on the board. Twice as many as you have people in the class. 6.14, 7.20, 9.45 etc.
Give each person in the class a number.
Then shout out a number at random and point to a time and the person who has that number has to give you the time. You can have the class in two teams if you wish. If a time is given correctly then that team gets one point.

Repeat until each person has given you two times.

This gives a lead-in to the theme of the unit 'No time'.

1 Routines

Aims
– to give students practice in asking and answering questions with 'How often …?'
– to practise the use of 'once', 'twice', 'three times'

a Write 'time' on the board. Ask students if they know another meaning of the word 'time' before you look at **1a**.

Give example sentences to clarify.
I clean my teeth 'twice a day'. – After breakfast and before I go to bed.
I go to a fitness studio on Friday and on Saturday. I go to a fitness studio 'two times'. – To elicit 'twice a week'.

Key 1a

once a day
twice a year / week / etc.
three times a month
three / four times a year / week / etc.

Ask students to complete the sentences:
I _____ once a day.
I _____ twice a day.
I _____ once a year / twice a year.
I _____ once a month / three times a month etc.

b,c Check comprehension of the word 'overtime'.

Then ask students to do task **1b** and to report back as in **1c**.

2 Routines in Maria's life

Aims
- to practise adverbs of frequency
- to help students to decide for themselves the meaning of them
- to focus on the word order with them
- to encourage students to express personal meaning using them

a Ask students to predict what Maria's answers might be to the questions in **2**. She is a mother and wife working in the twenty-first century. You will need to clarify the word 'century'.

This is by far the longest listening text that students have been exposed to up to this point in the book. It needs careful preparation.

1. Clarify: personal assistant, textile company, architect, overtime, conference (also be careful with the stress of this word – Ooo,) trade journal, venue, catering facilities.
2. Ask what sort of things a PA does for her boss (e.g. 'What do you think she does every day?, More than once a day? Once a week?').
3. Play up to: 'So what does a typical day look like?' Alert students to the fact that they have to listen for the first answer (two or three times a week).
4. Then stop the CD and ask students to predict when she starts and finishes work.
5. Then play the long passage in which Maria is talking about her day and alert the students that they have to listen for the answers to questions two (twice a day), three (once a week) and four (once a day – after lunch every day) – be careful: the words 'once a day' are not actually used!).
6. Then check.
7. Play the rest of the recording and ask students to listen for the answers to the final four questions. Check.
8. Play the whole recording again.

Tapescripts 2a / Track 11

I: Interviewer   M: Maria

I: Welcome to our programme "Ordinary People". In it we ask people, like you, the listeners, to talk about their working day in the twenty-first century. We want to answer the question: are routines different today? Maria is in our studio today and she is a wife and mother and also personal assistant to the manager of a small textile company. So Maria, how do you do it?

M: Good question! I suppose I organise my day carefully and I am lucky because my husband is an architect and he often works at home and my mum lives near us so they both help me with the children.

I: So when do you start and finish work?

M: Well, I start at 8.30 and officially I finish at 5.30.

I: Why do you say officially?

M: Well, I work overtime two or three times a week and if we have a big conference I work in the evening.

I: So what does a typical day look like?

M: At 8.30 I answer my e-mails and again at about 4.30. I still write some letters but most office communication is now by e-mail and once a week I book all flights and hotels for my boss online. I do that sort of thing in the morning. I also phone our partners in India or Hong Kong before lunch because the time there is eight hours ahead of us in the UK. I sometimes phone partners in Brazil and Mexico and that is, of course, in the afternoon. If I have a conference to organise I surf the net for information about venues and catering facilities. I read trade journals too after lunch and mark anything interesting for my boss. I don't have a lot of time to read during the week when I'm not in the office. I never read a newspaper. That's about it at the office I think.

I: A full day! When do you go shopping?

M: I go shopping for food once a week. Of course shops are open on Sundays in the UK so that's when I usually go shopping and with most supermarkets you can order groceries online, so I sometimes buy groceries that way.

I: And relaxation? Do you have time for that?

M: Not a lot! But I always try to listen to a music CD in the car on the way home and, oh, the children go swimming with Bob every Friday night and that's when I go to my yoga classes.

I: Your family is obviously important to you. How often do you go on holiday as a family?
M: We try to go away twice a year. We go skiing after Christmas, usually for a week, and then we always have a summer holiday with the children. We can't go on holiday when the children are in school so our main holiday is usually in July or August. It depends.
I: It sounds as though you deserve good holidays, Maria. Thank you.
M: Thank *you*.

Key 2a

1. 2-3 times a week
2. twice a day
3. once a week
4. once a day
5. once a week (on Sundays)
6. once a week (every Friday)
7. once a week (every Friday)
8. twice a year (skiing after Christmas and in the summer)

b Based on the text you have just listened to about Maria, how would you answer the question: 'Do you think routines are different now from routines in the 1990s?'
Prompt students to give a positive or negative reply as in the example sentences at the top of page 39 ('Yes, I think so.' / 'No, I don't think so.'). Encourage students to justify their opinions.

Also refer students to the **culture corner** at the bottom of page 38: 'Maria goes on holiday twice a year. Is that normal in your country?'

Background information
Workers in the UK are entitled to 20 days holiday a year under EU regulations. They are not entitled (though employers can allow it) to take the holiday they have not used in one year in the next one. The average worker in USA has only 13 days' holidays a year. If a public (or bank) holiday is at the weekend in Britain, workers get an extra day off to compensate for this. For example, in 2004 Christmas Day and Boxing Day were both at the weekend, so workers had Monday 27th and Tuesday 28th of December as holidays too.

Public holidays in Britain:

January 1st:	New Year's Day. In Scotland the new year celebrations are very important and are known as Hogmanay.
Good Friday	
Easter Monday	
May Day:	The May Day holiday is not always on May 1st as it is in the rest of Europe, but it is on the first Monday in May. In 2005 this was on May 2nd.
Spring Bank Holiday:	This usually falls near Whit Monday but in 2005 it was on May 30th, two weeks after Whit Monday.
Summer Bank Holiday:	Last Monday in August.
Christmas Day	
Boxing Day	

Federal holidays in USA:
There are ten Federal holidays in the USA.

January 1st:	New Year's Day.
January, third Monday:	Martin Luther King Day
February, third Monday:	President's Day
May, last Monday:	Memorial Day
July 4th:	Independence Day
September, first Monday:	Labor Day
October, second Monday:	Columbus Day
November 11th:	Veteran's Day
November, fourth Thursday:	Thanksgiving
December 25th:	Christmas Day

c Ask students to match the sentences from column A with ones from column B.

Suggestions:
twice a year = seldom
every day but not on Sunday = usually
no time to do it = never
every day after lunch = always
two or three times a week = often
once a month = seldom (you could ask whether the students think this is 'often' or 'sometimes')

Key 2c

1c; 2d; 3e; 4f; 5a; 6b

UNIT 4

d Focus on where the adverbs go in a sentence. Also point out that the order is different after the verb 'to be'.

Key 2d

1. seldom
2. always
3. often
4. usually
5. always; sometimes (x2)
6. never

e Ask students to complete the sentences so that they are true for them. Don't forget to ask them to write their sentences on a piece of paper.

Students are given the pattern and have to put their own ideas into this pattern. This ensures that the weaker students use the grammar correctly.

Collect in the pieces of paper and then re-distribute them so that each person has a piece of paper that doesn't belong to them.

Then ask students to read their new piece of paper. Who do they think wrote the sentences?
For example: I think this is Paula's paper because she likes swimming. This person often goes swimming.

Refer students to exercise **1** in the **back-up section** on page 46 for more work with adverbs of frequency.

Extra activity

If you want to give your students more practice in the use of adverbs of frequency and the question and answers with 'How often ...?', there is a **photocopiable board game on pages 46–47**.

Procedure

1. Divide the class into groups of three or four.
2. You will need a counter for each player – ask them to provide 1/2/5/10 cent pieces for this purpose.
3. You will need a dice for each group.
4. Copy one board (p. 46) for each group.
5. Copy one set of cards for each group.
6. Cut up the cards and put them in the appropriate place on the board.
7. To play: Throw the dice and move the appropriate number of places. If the player lands on a number, they are lucky, they do nothing!
   If they land on a ☐ square, they pick up a card and have to make a sentence with the adverb of frequency on the card. There are two jokers in this pile when they can use any adverb of frequency they like.
   If they land on a ○ square, they pick up a card and make a sentence with any adverb of frequency they like and the activity on the card.
   If they land on a △ square, they pick up a card and ask one person in their group a question with 'How often ...?' and the activity. Encourage students to continue this exchange as long as possible. So not just 'How often do you go to the cinema?' – 'Once a month.'
   See if they can ask additional questions, e.g. 'What sort of films do you like?' or 'Which is your favourite actor/actress?' etc. You may need to give an example of what you want here.
   Note: to the dentist's. Students may ask 'Why dentist's and not dentist?' Explanation: You go to the *place* where the dentist works, to the house *of* the dentist as it were.
8. The winner is the person who gets to the end first. Students have to throw the exact number needed to land on the *finish* square.

You might also like to teach some useful sentences for games at this point.
Whose turn is it?
It's your turn / my turn / his turn.

3 Work and stress

Aims
- to enjoy a song
- to encourage students to listen to what they *do* hear and understand in a song rather than what they don't
- to show students words that can collocate (go together)

Ask the question: Do you have a lot of stress at work?
Now you are going to listen to a song in which a woman has a lot of stress in her life.

Note
V.U. Headache: a headache that you get from sitting in front of a computer screen for a long time. A 'V(D)U' is a 'visual (display) unit'.

This is the first song in the book and there is a lot of work done on it *before* the students listen. This is deliberate for two reasons. Firstly, it is sung *fast* and so work needs to be done so that the first exposure to this sort of listening is a positive one. Secondly, it is meant to encourage students to concentrate on what they *do* hear/understand and not what they don't.

a,b Ask students to match a word from column A with one from column B and check with a partner. Check with the whole class. Then ask students to fill in the missing words from the song. Then play the song and the students check if they were right. This concentrates their attention on specific words.

Tapescripts 3b / Track 12

Get up, alarm clock, lip gloss, what a shock.
Get dressed, front door, more stress, what for?
Trapped in your world
You know you're trapped in your world
Lunch hour, fast food, telephone, more abuse.
V.U. headache, cigarettes, coffee break.
Trapped in your world
You know you're trapped in your world.
(Come out of the darkness)
Come out of the darkness, over the tower blocks
Into the light.
Go into the rush hour, out of the factory
Leave it behind
Turn on your TV. Back to suburbia, every night.
Come out of the darkness, over the offices, into the light.
(Come out of the darkness)
Leave work, happy hour, too drunk by far
Bus full, Waterloo, fall asleep on the tube.
Trapped in your world
You know you're trapped in your world.
(Come out of the darkness)

Vodka, lemonade, ashtrays, what a shame
Poor cow, sits alone, pubs close, go home.
Trapped in your world
You know you're trapped in your world.
(Come out of the darkness)
(by Republica)

Key 3a

alarm clock
get dressed
front door
coffee break
leave work
rush hour
go home
fast food
turn on your TV
fall asleep

Key 3b

clock, dressed, door, food, break, hour, on, TV, work, fall, home

c By now they should be quite familiar with the words of the song. Ask students to close their books. Play the song again and stop and ask students at random to predict what the *next* word will be.

Suggestions as to where to stop are indicated like this: //

Get up, alarm // clock, lip gloss, what a shock
Get // dressed, front // door, more stress, what for?
Trapped in your world
You know you're trapped in your world
Lunch // hour, fast food, telephone, more abuse
V.U. headache, cigarettes, coffee // break
Trapped in your world
You know you're trapped in your world.

(Come out of the darkness)
Come out of the darkness, over the tower blocks
Into the light
Go into the rush// hour, out of the factory
Leave it behind
(Come out of the darkness)
Turn on your TV, back to suburbia, every night
Come out of the // darkness, over the offices, into the // light
(Come out of the darkness)
Leave // work , happy // hour, too drunk by far
Bus full, Waterloo, fall // asleep on the tube
Trapped in your world
You know you're trapped in your world.

Vodka, // lemonade, ashtrays what a shame
Poor cow, sits alone, pubs // close, go // home
Trapped in your world
You know you're trapped in your // world.
(Come out of the darkness)

The person's routine:
Gets up (early), puts on her make-up (looks in the mirror early in the morning and doesn't like what she sees?!), leaves the house (You could speculate as to whether she has breakfast!), has a hamburger in her lunch hour and goes back to work where she answers the telephone, people ring her up and complain, she works on the computer and gets a headache. She smokes a lot and has a break in the afternoon. She leaves the factory when everyone else is leaving in the rush hour (between 5 and 6 in Britain). She always has a drink after work and is often drunk. She works in the city and lives in the suburbs. She is a commuter and gets to work by bus and tube. She either watches the TV alone or she goes to the pub on her own.

The **learning tip** extends the idea of concentrating on what you *do* hear rather than on what you don't. It is also useful to promote the idea of students doing some work outside the classroom. It is not really enough just to attend a course once or even twice a week. Students need to be given pointers as to how they can continue their learning outside the classroom. Sitting down and doing exercises from the **back-up section** is one way, of course, but listening to songs can be a more relaxing one.

4 Stress management

Aims
– to continue the theme of stress
– to give students practice in making and reacting to suggestions

a-c Look at the suggestions for combating stress.
Draw attention to the forms:
Why don't you ...?
You could ...
How about ...?

Take one or two examples from the list of suggestions in **4b** and drill with these three alternatives:

Put the following prompts on the board to elicit from the students:
'smile' – Why don't you smile? / You could smile. / How about smiling?
'go to a museum or art gallery' – You could go to a museum or art gallery. / Why don't you go to a museum or art gallery. / How about going to a museum or art gallery?
'have a massage' – You could have a massage. / How about having a massage? / Why don't you have a massage?

When the students make the suggestions respond either positively or negatively, so that they hear both ways of responding.

Then ask students to work in pairs and make and respond to suggestions.

d By asking students to choose *one* suggestion that they *both* agree on you are encouraging them to agree and disagree, to justify decisions.

Decide which stress busting idea the class agrees is the best.

If students enjoy reading, draw their attention to text **4** in the **Reading for fun section** which tells them something about the city of Bath, a spa in England which is famous for its hot springs.

4

5 Pronunciation

Aim
– to give students the opportunity to distinguish between the two sounds [e] and [æ]

a, b Students often confuse these two sounds because the [æ] sound doesn't exist in German. Before they can attempt to *make* the correct sound, students have to be able to *hear* the difference.

Play the CD and ask students to listen and repeat.

Tapescripts 5a / Track 13

1. men   –   man
2. ten   –   tan
3. bend –   band
4. send –   sand
5. pet   –   Pat
6. lend –   land

Tapescripts 5b / Track 14

men, ten, band, send, Pat, land

Then *you* say all the words at random and ask the students to raise their right hand if they hear the ones with [e] and their left hand if they hear the ones with [æ]. This has to be snappy or the point of the exercise is lost.
For example: man, men, man, lend, land, ten, bend, band, bend, band, land, pet, Pat, Pat, pet, send, sand, send, send, land, tan, ten, man, men, bend

c Then play **5c** and ask the students to write down the words they hear. This reinforces the spelling implications of the two sounds.

Tapescripts 5c / Track 15

1. I play in a rock band.
2. The man over there is my brother.
3. Be careful there is a dangerous bend in the road near here.
4. Linda hasn't got a pet.
5. You can get a tan in our sun studio.
6. Can you lend me some money?

Key 5c

1. band
2. man
3. bend
4. pet
5. tan
6. lend

The **learning tip** here encourages them to listen on their own at home so that they gradually get the feeling for which sound is which. Some students will feel more comfortable doing this sort of activity at home.

6 Sleep

Aims
– to clarify the notion of countable and uncountable nouns
– to give students practice in using questions with 'How much …?' and 'How many …?'

a Countable and uncountable nouns can be difficult for students to understand. The concepts that they have to master are those of mass or unit (countable or uncountable) and the general or the specific. Tasks 6 and 7 have been broken down into steps to help achieve this.

You as a teacher should keep the following in mind when using the material on pp. 42-43.
1. Distinguish between what you can count and what you can't count and so between the questions 'How much …?' and 'How many …?'
2. Understand the answers to these two questions that can be answered with a number or an amount, four as opposed to four litres (mass and unit).
3. Negative answers and questions without a determiner: 'I don't drink wine.' or 'Do you eat oranges?' ('wine' in this example is a general category of alcoholic drink)
4. The use of 'any' in questions and negatives with countable and uncountable nouns: 'There isn't any wine in the fridge.' In this example we are talking about the specific wine that I don't have.

Focus students' attention on the questions in red on page 42. Read them. You are surprised that the person only needs three hours sleep a night, hence the repetition of the question and 'How many …?' (the stress being on the 'How …?')

Ask students to read **6a** and fill in the missing information on questions with countable and uncountable nouns. The three questions that follow act as a check.

Key 6a

countable nouns – How many …?
uncountable nouns – How much …?

You can count 'glasses' of wine. You can't count wine.
You can count 'bottles' of gin. You can't count gin.
You can count 'litres' of water. You can't count water.

b Make up two questions from the table, one using 'much' and one using 'many' to clarify what the students have to do.

Give them enough time to make their questions and then demonstrate how to fill in the chart. Get the students to ask *you* a question each and give the answer.
Check that students understand which answers are appropriate drawing attention to your answers.

How many …?	Answer: write down a number.
How much …?	Answer: write down an amount, e.g. 3 bottles / two litres
I don't drink wine/gin.	Answer: put a cross

Key 6b

How much gin/water/herbal tea do you drink a day?
How many cups of coffee do you drink a day?
How much gin do you buy a week?
How many bottles of wine do you buy a week?

c Then ask students to stand up and ask three people in the group the questions. Do encourage them to stand up. This has two advantages. Firstly, it gives movement in the classroom to revive tired students and secondly, it encourages students to talk to people with whom they would not otherwise do so.

Report back stage.
Note: The answers here are: I don't drink wine. / I don't drink herbal tea. The use of 'any' in negative answers will come later. At this point we are looking at wine as a general class of alcoholic drink rather than a specific example of this that we might or might not have in our cupboard. Hence 'I don't drink wine' rather than 'I don't drink any wine'.

7 Food and your job

Aims
- to introduce and give students practice in the use of 'any' in questions and negative answers
- to make it clear when you use 'any' and when you can leave it out
- to give students practice in reading for information
- to introduce 'there is' and 'there are'

a Focus attention on the questions and Tim's answers to them. Then ask students to give their own answers.
If they answer 'yes', you can ask 'How much …?' or 'How many …?'

Then ask students to give their opinions about Tim's eating habits. Is it better to eat white bread or brown bread? Is it good to eat fish? Chips? Late at night?

b Then ask students to read the text on page 108 to find the answer to the question: 'Does Tim eat things that are good for him in his job?'

Before students read, clarify the following words: brain, stamina, improve, memory.

If students ask, you can also clarify 'FAQ' (frequently asked questions), but this is not necessary to be able to successfully complete this task.

Note: This is a fictional home-page, but it is based on two genuine web-sites on which doctors offer advice and send regular newsletters to people who are on the mailing list.

Key 7b

Tim doesn't eat brown bread, fish or nuts. – This is not very good for his brain. But he eats oranges.

Tim sometimes eats chips and he sometimes eats his dinner late at night (at 8.30 or 9p.m.). – He should be careful because this can affect his concentration level and his sleep.

c We now go from the general to the specific.

Tim doesn't eat nuts. So there aren't any nuts in his kitchen.
He doesn't eat fish. So there isn't any fish in his fridge.

Draw attention to the difference between 'there aren't' and 'there isn't'. Ask students to think about the difference. You use 'there isn't' with uncountable nouns and 'there aren't' with countable ones.

If you feel that it is necessary to drill your students before they go to do the pair work task, proceed as follows.

Write the following list on the board:
coffee
herbal tea
nuts
bread
butter
apples
chocolate
eggs
meat
sausages
gin
water
beer

Ask students to pose questions to you to find out what you have in your kitchen.
Is there any ...?
Are there any ...?

You reply 'Yes, there is. / No, there isn't. / No, there aren't. / Yes, there are.' as appropriate.

Then ask students to do the task in pairs. Student A looks on page 44 and student B at the **file section** on page 110.

Note
English usage is changing and 'There's ...' (there is) is often used with a plural subject in spoken English, e.g.
There's a problem with this.
There's some problems with this.

It is for this reason that we have not given weight to the practising of positive sentences such as:
There's some meat in the fridge.
There are some nuts in the cupboard.

Refer students to the **back-up section** exercises **2** and **3** for more work with countable and uncountable nouns.

d Now students tell the class what there is in their kitchen cupboard/fridge. Ask them to explain why.

8 Making a booking

Aims
– to give students practice in using the telephone to make bookings
– to reinforce spelling
– to show how you can ask for clarification if you don't understand something on the phone
– to use the questions 'How much ...?' and 'How many ...?' from the unit in an everyday life situation

Encourage students to make an attempt at filling in the missing information for themselves and then check the answers.

Tapescripts 8 /Track 16-17

1. ▲ Lotus restaurant. Can I help you?
   ● I'd like to book a table for six for Friday 13th February at 1 p.m., please.
   ▲ Sorry, for how many people?
   ● 6.
   ▲ Er – let me see. Yes, that's fine. Can I have your name, please?
   ● The table is for Mr Sutcliffe. That's S-U-T-C-L-I-F-F-E.
   ▲ Fine. That's a table for six on Friday 13th February at 1p.m.
   ● Thanks very much.
   ▲ Not at all. Goodbye.

2. ▲ Hilton Hotel Heathrow Airport. Can I help you?
   ● I'd like to book a small conference room for the morning of the 4th July.
   ▲ For how many people?
   ● About fifteen.
   ▲ Sorry, was that fifty or fifteen?
   ● Fifteen.
   ▲ I'm sorry, madam, but the small conference rooms are not available then. One small one is free in the afternoon or there's one that seats fifty that's free in the morning.
   ● No, I really need a small one for the morning but thanks anyway.
   ▲ Not at all. Goodbye.
   ● Goodbye.

Allow students to listen and check the answers. Then ask them to work in pairs and act out the dialogues.
If you have a pair that would be willing to perform in front of the class, ask them to do so. You could at this point do some work on intonation if necessary. With the word 'Sorry?' as an indication that you want some information repeated, the intonation goes up.

Another way of making the intonation clear is to encourage your students to look down and then up, chin down and then chin up as they say 'Sorry'.

Back-up section

Mention has been made at appropriate points as to what back-up activities are appropriate.
If students have done the vocabulary task **4** (3), you could have this as a warmer for the following lesson.

Possible words in square 3:
air, arch, art, act, ache, architect, ate, chat, cheat, chart, cart, cat, car, eat, each, ear, earth, hat, hit, hire, hair, hare, heart, heat, ice, itch, race, rat, reach, rich, rice, tar, tea, tear, tire, treat, trace, tract, teach

Photocopiable worksheets for unit 4, extra activity

START	2	▢	◯
	▢ CARDS		5
△	◯	7	△
▢		◯ CARDS	
11	△	◯	14
	△ CARDS		▢
FINISH	◯	△	16

Photocopiable worksheets for unit 4, extra activity

Cards for ☐

always	sometimes	usually	often
seldom	never	joker	joker

Cards for

work overtime	drink champagne for breakfast	eat meat	drink gin
ride a bike to work	listen to music	watch TV	go swimming
work in the garden	wear something green	listen to music	have a massage
get drunk	drink red wine	drink beer	go to bed after midnight

Cards for

go to the theatre	go to the cinema	do some sort of sport	clean your teeth
see your family	visit friends	go out to a restaurant	go to the dentist's
write letters to friends	go away for the weekend	have a family holiday	go shopping

© 2005 Max Hueber Verlag
This sheet may be photocopied and used within the class.

UNIT 5 Communication

Topics:	In this unit students talk about modern forms of communication.
Vocabulary:	describing people and events; shopping; sections in a newspaper
Structures:	present progressive for descriptions and to talk about what is happening now; adverbs of manner; linking words in sentences
Functions:	expressing opinions and responding politely
Skills:	reading for gist in an e-mail; reading for detail and guessing unknown words in a newspaper article; writing a simple text message
Pronunciation:	listening for the difference in the two sounds [tʃ] and [dʒ]; sentence stress in short answers
Job Talk:	saying 'no' politely; telephone expressions
Culture corner:	events in different countries (e.g. carnival)
Learning tip:	reading and predicting words you may read
Reading for fun:	Text number 5 talks about Shrove Tuesday or Pancake Day in England.
Time considerations:	lesson 1: 1 and 2 (with a good group maybe 3 – gist reading only and then the more detailed reading to pick out the adverbs could be done at home)
	lesson 2: 3c and 3d, 4 and 5 and (6a)
	lesson 3: (6) 7 and 8 and 9

If you are short of time you can leave out 6. Those students who use English for their job will find 7 and 8 a lot more relevant to them than 6. You could also leave out 9a as students can do the reading task in 9c without knowing the words for the newspaper sections.

Warmer

The mobile phone line-up
Ask one student the question 'How often do you use your mobile phone?' Then have all students ask each other the same question and to line up at the front of the classroom in the order 'ten times a day' at the far right of the line, for example, and at the far left of the line 'once a month' or 'never' if someone doesn't have a mobile phone.
Ask the students then to sit down with the person next to them in the line. This person will be their partner.

1 Modern communication

Aims
– to introduce the topic of modern communication
– to review the question 'How often ...?'
– to give students practice in reading for information

a Ask the questions in **1a**. Say students are going to read a text about mobile phones.
Write the following words on the board: satellite, fashion accessory, passenger, aerials, colour, tram. What do the words tell you about mobile phones? This predicting activity lightens the reading load.

Then ask the students to do the reading task and then check the answers with a partner and finally with the whole class.

Key 1a

1. true   4. false / possible
2. true   5. true / possible
3. false   6. possible

b Ask the questions in **1b** and also ask what ringing tones people in your class have for their mobile phone and if they change the colour every day or every week as it says in the text.

2 Family photos

Aims
- to introduce the present progressive used for descriptions and temporary situations
- to give practice in listening for specific information

a On the first listening ask students to listen for the names and the descriptions so that they can label the picture. Not all the people are mentioned in the first picture (on the right). Point out that two people are described in this picture and two in the one underneath it in which the people are sitting down.

Tapescripts 2a / Track 18

Rachel: Who are all these people? They all look very dressed up.
Clare: Well, yes, of course they are. The photos were taken on Pamela and Andy's wedding day. Well, let's see. The woman who's wearing this turquoise dress and this fabulous hat is my mum, you don't know her, do you?
Rachel: No, I don't. And who's the man next to Andy?
Clare: Oh, you mean the man who's wearing the dark suit and dark red tie? That's Simon.
Rachel: Ah, right, is he still living in that bachelor flat in London?
Clare: Oh no. He's married now and he and his wife Kate are renting a flat in Windsor. They want to buy a house but everything is so expensive.
Rachel: Yeah, I know. And who are the people in this next picture? Who's the man with the dark grey suit and the blue tie?
Clare: That's Roger!
Rachel: Gosh that's Roger? I don't recognise him. How old is he now?
Clare: 24. He's in Rio at the moment. He and a friend are travelling round the world in his gap year after university and before he starts work.
Rachel: And the woman sitting next to him? Is that his girlfriend Natalie?
Clare: Yeah, that's right. That dress looks good on her, doesn't it? Pink suits her.
Rachel: Yeah, it does. And is she travelling with him?
Clare: Not at the moment. She's training to be a nurse and she can't interrupt her course. They may meet in Mexico after her exams.
Rachel: Remember me to them if you are in contact by e-mail.
Clare: Yeah, I will.

b Then play the CD again and ask students to answer the questions in **2b**. Which sentences are used as descriptions and which are used to talk about a temporary action?
('She's wearing this turquoise dress.' is the only description.)

Key 2b

She's wearing a turquoise hat.	Mum
He's living in Windsor with his new wife.	Simon
He's travelling round the world.	Roger
She's studying to be a nurse.	Natalie

When they have finished and done the listening task you can ask the students to look at the tapescript (see above) and pick out more examples of descriptions and temporary actions.

Focus on the form. Look at the example sentences (underlined). These are not permanent situations, they will finish sometime soon in the future. We call this tense the present progressive or the present continuous because it talks about an action that is continuing or that is still in progress.

UNIT 5   49

c Explain the words: 'decorating/renovating the house/flat' and then ask students to circulate to find out how many people answer 'yes' to their questions. Give an example of question and answer.
Are you reading a good book at the moment? – Yes, I am. / No, I'm not.
Are you trying to lose weight? – Yes, I am. / No, I'm not.

If you have someone who may feel uncomfortable answering the question about losing weight, it might be better to have this as the plenary question. Then this person is not embarrassed many times by being asked the question over and over again.

Report back.

3 You've got an e-mail

Aims
- to reinforce the use of the present progressive for a temporary action
- to introduce the adverbs of manner
- to give students practice in gist reading

a Ask if your students still send postcards when they are on holiday or do they send messages from an Internet café?

b Ask students to read the mail quickly and to decide what event is taking place (it is Carnival in Rio). Then clarify any problems with vocabulary. Try to encourage students to guess the words as far as possible.

humid	Rio is in South America. What is the weather like there? (the German word?)
to get used to it	Something was difficult or a problem but it isn't now.
cheering	Fans cheer when their football team is winning.
drag queen	Use the pictures to help you.
procession	Again try to elicit the answer. What happens at 'Fasching' or 'Carnival' in the area where you live? What do you see in the streets on 'Rosenmontag' in Cologne and Mainz?
crowds	A lot of people.
wigs	Hair that is not your hair.
jewellery	(elicit) Show a ring.
feathers	Draw some.
complain	When the service is not good in a hotel you ...
pick-pockets	People who try to steal your money in a big mass of people are ...

Ask about 'Fasching' or 'Mardi Gras' (fat Tuesday) or 'Carnival' (farewell to meat) in your area. What happens? Are there celebrations on Monday and Tuesday before Ash Wednesday?

If students enjoy reading and are interested in the topic of carnival, text number 5 in the **Reading for fun section** on **page 111** talks about Shrove Tuesday.

c Now that the students understand the contents of the e-mail ask them to look at it again and this time to pick out the words that end in **-ly**.

Key 3c

Thousands of people are singing and cheering enthusiasti**cally** and dancing wild**ly**.
The drag queens dress outrageous**ly**.
No-one is shouting or complaining loud**ly**.

Tell students that these are adverbs. They describe a verb or an adjective and answer the question 'How ...?'
What is the music like? – Loud.
How is the band playing? – Loudly.

Ask students to match the verbs with the adverbs they have found in the text.

d Then draw attention to **3d**. Adverbs can go together with more than one verb.

Key 3d

cheering	wildly, enthusiastically, loudly, noisily
singing	loudly, beautifully, noisily, quietly, enthusiastically
laughing	loudly, <u>nervously</u>, <u>happily</u>
dancing	<u>enthusiastically</u>, wildly
jeering	loudly, noisily, angrily, wildly
waiting	patiently, nervously
crying	<u>loudly</u>, <u>quietly</u>, noisily

shouting	loudly, <u>noisily</u>, wildly, angrily
playing	carefully, dangerously (a sport), <u>loudly</u>, <u>quietly</u> (an instrument)
screaming	loudly, wi<u>ldly</u>, noisily

Ask students if they can add any other adverbs to the list given in **3d**. Some good students may already know one or two more but avoid giving students a long list as you can easily overload them at this level. A couple of suggestions are underlined in the list above.

4 An exciting event

Aims
- to allow students to do some writing
- to review short forms used in text messages
- to review adverbs and the present progressive

Divide the students into groups of three or four, but not more.

One way of getting them into groups would be to find postcards that depict a lot of action. Cut each postcard into three or four, distribute them and students have to find their group by finding the people who have the other pieces of the postcard. They do this by asking the questions: 'What do you think is happening in your postcard?' Put the students into groups *first* and *then* explain the task, otherwise they will forget what they have to do.

Explain that they are at an important event. They are going to send a text message to their friends about this event. So in the **files section** on pages 107, 108, 113, 114, there are four events, so enough for twelve and a maximum of sixteen students. If you have classes that are bigger than 16 students, have two groups working on the same event.

Give an example: If they were at a pop festival a message might look like this:
It is GR8 here. There are thousands of PPL here all sleeping in tents over the weekend. It isn't raining ☺ ☺ so we are sitting on the grass listening and singing along with the music very enthusiastically and of course drinking beer. RU watching this on TV? G2G. A new band is coming on to the stage. CYA soon.

Then ask students to compose their own text message. Be on hand to help with vocabulary if necessary. If groups have no idea of any abbreviations to use in the text message don't insist on it! Let them write what they would do in a postcard. Make sure they understand they shouldn't write in the example: 'Hello, we are here enjoying the pop festival.' That would mean there was no point in guessing what the event was.

When groups have finished the writing phase, collect in their texts and give them to another group. This new group has to guess what the event is. Allow time for discussion in groups and then, in plenary, ask groups to share their guesses.

Refer students to the **back-up section** exercises **3** and 4 which give extra practice in the present simple or the present continuous and adverbs and adjectives.

5 Are they cheering or jeering?

Aim
- to give students practice in distinguishing between the sounds [tʃ] and [dʒ]

a If sounds are confused it doesn't always lead to misunderstanding, but with these two sounds it *is* important to differentiate between them.

It is not necessary to give help with the vocabulary first as the aim is simply to listen for the *sound*.

Tapescripts 5a / Track 19

[tʃ]		[dʒ]
1. cherry	–	Jerry
2. cheap	–	jeep
3. choke	–	joke
4. chill	–	Gill
5. chest	–	jest
6. chin	–	gin
7. choose	–	Jews
8. cheer	–	jeer

Then you can clarify vocabulary if students want to know the meaning of the words. Try as far as possible to elicit meaning. Try to avoid just giving the answer in German. It doesn't help those students whose mother tongue isn't German and it doesn't force any students to think for themselves.

cherry	small red, round fruit
cheap	not expensive
jeep	an SUV (sport utility vehicle – car enthusiasts will know this abbreviation), a sort of Land Rover
choke	demonstrate it
chill	in the winter if you don't wear warm clothes you get a …
chest	point to it
jest	another word for: to have a laugh
chin	point to it
choose	demonstrate (show two pens, for example, and say 'You choose')
cheer	to shout 'Hooray'
jeer	to shout 'BOOO'

b, c Then play the CD again and students listen for the words they hear to tick the words in column A or B.

Play the CD a third time and students answer the four questions with words from column A.

Tapescripts 5b / Track 20

cherry, cheap, joke, Gill, chest, gin, choose, jeer

Tapescripts 5c / Track 21

Gill is in bed with a chill.
Jerry is eating a cherry.
The jeep is cheap.
The Turin fans are cheering and the Manchester United fans are jeering.

6 Shopping and the Internet

Aims
- to give students the opportunity to give opinions in a limited way
- to encourage students to use clues to sort out two short dialogues
- to widen students' vocabulary in the lexical field of clothes

a Ask students to read the uses of the Internet and decide which apply to them so that you can come up with a class profile. How does the class use the Internet?

b Then ask students to work in groups of three or four. Give each person in the group a letter A, B, C, D. Either display the following on the board or give a copy of it to each group.

1. Person A gives his or her opinion about sentence one.
   Person B agrees or disagrees with A.
   Person C (and D) agree(s) or disagree(s) with B.

2. Person B gives his or her opinion about sentence two.
   Person C (and person D) agree(s) or disagree(s) with B.
   Person A agrees or disagrees with C and D.

3. Person C (and person D) give(s) his or her opinion about sentence three.
   Person A agrees or disagrees with C and D.
   Person B agrees or disagrees with A.

This is very mechanical but it ensures that everyone has a turn at giving an opinion and then agreeing or disagreeing. It is very controlled for students at this level.

c Ask if the students like shopping! Do they always try something on before they buy it?
They are going to complete two dialogues. Point out that in one dialogue someone buys a shirt and in the other someone wants to buy two pullovers. To assemble the dialogues they have to sort out the sentences. Show them how they can decide which sentences belong to which dialogue. For example: If the customer is buying a shirt will the question be: 'Can I try them on?' or 'Can I try it on?'
Ask students to work in pairs or groups and sort out the dialogues. Some students find it easier to do this sort of exercise if they can actually move the sentences around. If your students would like to do this look at the **photocopiable worksheet on page 56**. Copy one worksheet for each group and cut the sentences into strips.

Tapescripts 6c / Track 22

Dialogue 1

Sales assistant:	Can you find the colour you want, madam?
Customer:	Do you have these pullovers in red?
Sales assistant:	Yes, we do. Here you are. Would you like to try them on?
Customer:	Yes, please.

Sales assistant: The fitting rooms are over there.
(pause)
Customer: They are a bit small. Have you got a bigger size?
Sales assistant: No, I'm sorry, we haven't.
Customer: Oh, well, I'll leave it then.

Dialogue 2
Sales assistant: Are you looking for a shirt to go with those trousers, sir?
Customer: Yes, I am.
Sales assistant: Any particular colour?
Customer: Have you got anything in green?
Sales assistant: How about this one?
Customer: Yes, it's nice. Can I try it on?
Sales assistant: Certainly. The fitting rooms are over there.
(pause)
Customer: Yes, it fits very well. How much is it?
Sales assistant: £23.
Customer: Fine, I'll take it.

When the students have completed the task allow them to listen to check if they were right. Then ask them to practise with a partner.

Refer students to exercise **2** in the **back-up section** on page 56 for more work on vocabulary and clothes.

7 I'm sorry, we haven't

Aims
– to alert students to the rhythm of a sentence
– to reinforce the use of 'sorry' for an apology

This activity is appropriate for those using English at work, but also for those who use it on holiday or for pleasure.

a The circles filled in represent the words or syllables that are stressed. Stressing the right words and syllables gives English its rhythm.

b As with sounds, some students have difficulty *hearing* the correct rhythm. To make it clearer for such students knock on the desk with a knuckle for the unstressed words and syllables and with the palm of your hand for the stressed ones and ask them to decide which pattern the sentences represent.

Key 7b
1. A
2. B
3. B
4. B
5. A
6. A
7. B
8. A

c Then ask students to match the answers with the questions and listen for the correct answers.

Key 7c
1. I'm sorry, I don't.
2. I'm sorry, I'm not.
3. I'm sorry, it isn't.
4. I'm sorry, you can't.
5. I'm sorry, there isn't.
6. I'm sorry, it doesn't.
7. I'm sorry, I can't.
8. I'm sorry, we haven't.

Then play the CD, stop it after the questions and ask students to give you the answer, paying particular attention to the rhythm.

Tapescripts 7c / Track 23

Do you know his phone number? – I'm sorry, I don't.
Are you free on Sunday? – I'm sorry, I'm not.
Is the rental car insured for my wife? – I'm sorry, it isn't.
Can I smoke in here? – I'm sorry, you can't.
Excuse me, is there an Internet café near here? – I'm sorry, there isn't.
Excuse me, does this bus stop at the main station? – I'm sorry, it doesn't.
Can you give me a lift to the airport? – I'm sorry, I can't.
Have you got a double room free for tonight? – I'm sorry, we haven't.

If you want to give the students extra practice, you will need a ball that doesn't bounce. Read a question and throw the ball to a student who has to give the appropriate response. Then ask this student to choose another question and throw the ball to another student who has to give the response and so on.

8 Telephone expressions

Aims
- to introduce and practise some expressions useful for use on the phone
- to reinforce the use of 'sorry'
- to reinforce the use of the present progressive for activities that are of limited duration
- to reinforce the pronunciation of 'Can ...?' in questions

a This activity is primarily of relevance to students who use English for their job and can be omitted if students are not interested in English used in the office.

What do you say when you are on the phone (to say who you are)? – 'Ms Braun here.' or 'This is Ms Braun.' (*not:* Here Ms Braun.)
What does a secretary say if the boss is not there? – 'Can I take a message?'
Note: The *caller* says 'Can I leave a message?' and the person taking the call says 'Can I take a message?'

Explain the word 'urgent'.

Let students fill in the missing words and then play the CD to check.

Tapescripts 8a / Track 24

1. ▲ This is Michael Grundy. Can I speak to Mr. Sutton, please?
   ● I'm sorry, he's having lunch at the moment. Can I take a message?
   ▲ It's OK. It's not urgent. I'll ring back later.
   ● Fine.

2. ▲ This is Charles Morton. Can I speak to Mr Archer, please?
   ● I'm sorry, he's attending a conference in Rome at the moment. Can I take a message?
   ▲ It's rather urgent. Can I have his mobile number?

   ● Of course. It's 01717 480567.
   ▲ Thank you for your help.
   ● Not at all. Goodbye.

b If you wish students to make up their own dialogues, you could have a brainstorming session as to how many ways you can complete the sentence:

I'm sorry he's ... | attending a conference.
 | in a meeting.
 | off sick (ill and so at home).
 | in hospital.
 | visiting a factory / a supplier.

9 What's in the news?

Aims
- to widen students' vocabulary in the lexical field of newspapers
- to encourage learners to guess meaning from context

a Ask the questions. Students should guess which sections are relevant from the clues in the sentences. Some they will know and some they should be encouraged to guess.

You may need to clarify certain words.
ordinary   Not special. Ordinary people are people like you and me.
developments   Things that are new.

Then check the answers.

Key 9a

1. sports
2. gossip column
3. home news
4. entertainment pages
5. human interest
6. business and the economy
7. science and technology
8. world news

Then clarify any more vocabulary that is necessary.

b This comes from the human interest or business section. Which do the students think?

If you receive regular junk mail, bring it in to the class before you throw it away. This may stimulate students' imaginations to talk about the junk mail they have. Do they get irritated or angry about junk mail? This is a good opportunity to clarify the word 'irritated' that is in the first paragraph of the text.

What do you think the title tells you. What *can* you do about junk mail apart from throw it away?

c Ask students to read the questions *before* they read the text. Clarify that Bovingdon is the name of a village and Hertfordshire is the name of a county (bigger than a German 'Landkreis' and smaller than a 'Bundesland'). Bourne End is a village and Tring is a town both near Bovingdon, and Reading is a town near Oxford. The other word you should clarify before the students begin to read is 'suing'.

Don't let the students be irritated by the missing information in the text. The text makes perfect sense without them.

Allow them to read the text, answer the questions and then compare them with a partner.

Key 9c

1. He's trying to do something about all the junk mail he gets every week and he's also trying to help people with junk mail.
2. People write about junk mail stories and ask for help.
3. Companies who are trying to sell trekking holidays.
4. In Tring.
5. In Reading.
6. He's a computer programmer. He runs a web-site.
7. She can register with the Mailing Preference Service (www.mpsonline.org.uk).
8. www.readgroup.co.uk
9. No web-site can help them with their legal problems.
10. No, he throws them into the dustbin.

You can then ask the students what they think about the ideas for stopping junk mail. Do you still get e-mail for people who have moved from your address in Germany? Why not?

Background information
The system of registration is very different in Britain. You don't have to register with the authorities when you move house and you don't change the registration of your car. It is easier for authorities in Germany to know who lives at what address and avoids the problem that Peter Moran has. When a census is taken every ten years then the authorities know how many people are living at a certain address. This is the information that people use when they are trying to find out about their family history.

d Then ask students to fill in the missing words.

Key 9d

1. four-week
2. who is 95
3. children's
4. 32-year old
5. expensive

Back-up section

The vocabulary revision exercise in the back-up involves learners reading sentences very carefully to spot the mistakes. The Guardian newspaper, a quality daily, is sometimes called the Grauniad because it often has spelling mistakes in it! Other quality newspapers are: The Daily Telegraph, The Times, The Independent. The Daily Telegraph is the only paper that is still published in what is called the broadsheet format (very large). The Times is now published in tabloid format and the others in a size in between the two.
Tabloid newspapers: The Sun (the most popular newspaper in Britain), The Daily Express, The Daily Mail.

Reference to revision unit

If your students need more work on adverbs, look at the listening section of the revision unit on page 76.

Photocopiable worksheet for unit 5, 6c

Can you find the colour you want, madam?
Yes, please.
The fitting rooms are over there.
They are a bit small. Have you got a bigger size?
Are you looking for a shirt to go with those trousers, sir?
Yes, it's nice. Can I try it on?
Certainly. The fitting rooms are over there.
How about this one?
Fine, I'll take it.
No, I'm sorry, we haven't.
Oh, well, I'll leave it then.
Do you have these pullovers in red?
Yes, we do. Here you are. Would you like to try them on?
Yes, it fits very well. How much is it?
£23.
Yes, I am.
Any particular colour?
Have you got anything in green?

UNIT 6 On holiday

Topics:	In this unit students talk about holiday experiences.
Vocabulary:	hotels of the world and facilities in them
Structures:	comparative and superlative of adjectives; past simple of 'to be' and regular verbs; questions in the past simple; conjunctions
Functions:	expressing sympathy, surprise and enthusiasm; making a booking
Skills:	listening for detail in a dialogue; reading for detail in short texts about hotels, in a postcard and in on-line booking details
Pronunciation:	sounding friendly
Learning tip:	practising new words
Reading for fun:	Texts 6, 7, 8: The great British breakfast, The holiday postcard, The Guinness book of records
Time considerations:	lesson 1: 1-3 (This will depend on how enthusiastic students are with task 2. This *could* take quite a long time and so not allow you to finish 3. You would not have time to do the extra activity in this first lesson of the new unit either.)
	lesson 2: 4-6 (6 is optional, particularly if not many of your students have access to the Internet. The reading skills practised are useful, particularly if students are interested in taking exams, but leaving it out does not affect the grammar or vocabulary of the unit to a great extent.)

Warmer

If you want to review vocabulary from the previous unit you can use the **photocopiable worksheet on page 64** for this purpose. This is in the form of a memory game. Copy it and cut up into words and pictures. On the reverse side of the ten picture cards write numbers from 1-10 and on the reverse side of the word cards mark letters A-J.

Card A *should not* form a pair with card 1 and B should not form a pair with 2 etc. Place the cards face down on a table. Students then, in groups of three, play memory with them. One students picks up one letter card and one number card. If these two cards form a pair, the student keeps them. Then it is the next student's turn. If a student is unsuccessful at finding a pair, he/she places the cards back face down and the next student has a turn. The person with the most pairs at the end of the game wins.

To form a link with this warmer and the topic of the lesson ask 'What sort of clothes do you wear when you are on holiday?'

1 Where to stay?

Aims
- to give students practice in reading for information
- to encourage shyer students to talk
- to introduce the comparative and superlative forms of adjectives

a Look at the pictures. Where do students think these hotels are? Ask them to speculate how much you would pay a night to stay in one of them. Do they stay in expensive hotels when they're on holiday? Probably not! Where can you stay? Complete **1a**.

Key 1a

On holiday you can stay in a: hotel, Bed & Breakfast, guest house, tent, caravan or mobile home, holiday flat, rented flat, youth hostel or on a campsite.

UNIT 6   57

6

b-d Today students are going to read about *very* expensive hotels.
Divide the students into three groups. Make sure that no group is made up of only very strong students or only weak ones. Have roughly the same number in each group.

Procedure
1. Before you begin clarify the following: health and recreation facilities.

2. Groups read their texts and, on page 58, fill in the information about their hotel. The three groups have different texts but all the students in each group have the same text.
Be on hand to help with more vocabulary if necessary. The idea of having mixed ability groups for this task is so that weaker students can be supported by their stronger peers before they have to talk about their own text in stage 4.
As the students are reading in their groups give each member of the three groups a number. If you have a number of students in your class that doesn't divide by 3, you will need to have a couple of groups of four in stage 4, in which case give two people in one or two groups the same number at this stage.

3. Ask students to find their two partners, the people with the same number as they have.

4. In this phase the three students in the new groups all have *different* texts and so everyone is forced to speak. Students exchange information so that they can fill in the details of the other two hotels.

When students have exchanged their information you can clarify any vocabulary that the students are still unsure of if necessary and ask the students which hotel they would like to stay in if money were no problem!

These three expensive hotels have been chosen so that the comparison is a realistic one. It is not sensible to compare a cheap hotel with an expensive one and say: 'Hotel X is more expensive than hotel Y.'

Focus on **1d** and the way you form the comparative and superlative of adjectives.
What about shorter adjectives?
What's the opposite of 'expensive'? – Cheap.
Then show the comparative and superlative of this short adjective: cheap, cheaper, cheapest.

Look at the **grammar box** on page 59 and draw attention to the spelling after adjectives that end in -y.

Work on comparatives has been limited to the comparative and superlative positive form and so expressions like 'as ... as' or 'not as ... as' have been omitted at this level.

Now ask for some more comparisons based on the hotels.

You can help with questions or allow students to make comparisons for themselves.
Which is the biggest?
The smallest?
The furthest from the airport?
Which has got the best sports facilities?
Where do you think you could have the most interesting holiday?

2 Can you recommend a hotel?

Aims
– to give students practice in using comparative and superlative adjectives
– to give a reason to write

It is important when writing to have some reason to do so. This is why the students write and look at each other's efforts. If you feel that students will not know much about hotels and restaurants in their area because they never stay in them and they only go out to one favourite restaurant, give them some warning that you need some information about local hotels and restaurants and ask them to go and find some brochures or to find some information on-line about them.

Extra activity
If your students want to do more talking, this activity is called a pyramid discussion and encourages students to justify their ideas. It can be useful for students who use English at work, as the categories could be applied to a business hotel and not just a holiday one.

Copy the **photocopiable worksheet on page 65** so that every student has a copy of the features of a hotel. (So copy 1 worksheet per two students in your class. Cut the worksheet in half.)

Students decide for themselves which five features, either from the list or including two of their own, are important to them. They then join another

UNIT 6

group and *as a group* have to come to a new decision, a new list of five features that all the members of the group can agree on. Finally you bring all the students together and arrive at a class decision. At this stage you will be encouraging students to use comparative and superlative forms: 'The most important feature for our group is …' / 'For us a clean hotel is more important than a luxurious one.'

Exercise **3** on page 65 of the **back-up section** gives students more practice with comparatives and superlatives. Ask students to bring their ideas to the next lesson.

3 Honeymoon in Hong Kong

Aims
- to introduce the simple past of the verb 'to be'
- to give practice in listening for specific information
- to widen vocabulary
- to draw students' attention to nouns and adjectives that can collocate (go together)

a Before you begin clarify the following expressions.

'Was it worth it?' / 'It was worth every penny.' – It was expensive, but it was good value for money. (Obviously the original expression uses 'penny' because of it being English, but you pay in dollars in Hong Kong, of course.)
'You can say that again.' – It emphasises that you agree 100% with what the first speaker has just said. (in German: Das kannst du laut sagen.)
'What a shame!' – You say this when you are sorry about something bad that happened. German learners often think that it translates as 'eine Schande' (a disgrace) rather than 'schade'.

Background information
The outside of the Peninsular Hotel Hong Kong (pictured on page 59) was often seen in the American soap opera 'Dynasty' ('The Denver Clan') when Blake Carrington and Alexis Colby were plotting new ways to get richer from the South China Sea oil wells.

Before you play the CD point out that Anna is in Britain again when she rings her friend. The holiday in Hong Kong is finished so she talks in the past tense. Then draw attention to the questions.

Key 3a

1. The room was on the 15th floor.
2. The view was spectacular.
3. The people were friendly and helpful.
4. The flight was long and uncomfortable.

The first three pieces of information are contained in quite a long speech by Anna. Students have to concentrate, but concentrate on specific words and don't concentrate on all the peripheral words that they may or may not know.

Tapescripts 3a / Track 25

Pat: 6267887
Anna: Hi, Pat. This is Anna.
Pat: Anna! You're back. Did you have a good time?
Anna: Oh Pat, it was wonderful.
Pat: So what was the hotel like? Was it worth all that money?
Anna: Every penny – well, every dollar. Our room was on the fifteenth floor and the view over the harbour was really spectacular, the food was good, all the people in the hotel were always friendly and helpful.
Pat: Well, you sound happy. When did you arrive back?
Anna: Yesterday.
Pat: How's the jet lag?
Anna: Bad! It was a long uncomfortable flight. We didn't sleep very well so we were very tired when we arrived back.
Pat: Oh, that's a shame. A bed at The Peninsular is more comfortable than a seat on a Boeing 747, I suppose!
Anna: You can say that again. By the way, did you get the postcard?
Pat: No.
Anna: That's strange, I posted it ten days ago. Never mind. Look, can we meet up sometime next week so that I can tell you all about it?
Pat: Sure. How about Monday?
Anna: Fine, see you then.
Pat: Great. Bye.
Anna: Bye.

6

When they have picked out the information, draw attention to the questions 'What was … like?" and 'What were … like?'. If you need to check that the concept has been understood, you can drill here. Give prompts and the students have to decide which is the appropriate question: food, hotel, people, facilities, bars, swimming pool, beach, weather, night life, shops.

Once you have introduced these two questions you have an ideal opportunity to have some real meaningful communication in the classroom. If a student has been away on holiday, encourage his or her fellow students to ask as many questions with 'What was/were the … like?' It is important that students and not *you* ask these questions. It then becomes a routine. You can also extend the question to 'What was your weekend like?'

b Clarify any unknown words.

spicy Give an example of a spice, e.g. curry, paprika, chilli. Also point out that food with a lot of chilli could be hot.
humid hot and wet
noisy German students often use the word 'loud' to translate: 'Es war sehr laut.' It is important to show that the choice of appropriate adjective depends on the noun with which it collocates. So a voice can be loud but not noisy, but a room is noisy and not loud.

Key 3b

hotel	very comfortable, expensive, good, dirty, clean
beach	dirty, clean, sandy
people	noisy, helpful, friendly
food	spicy, boring, hot, international
rooms	very comfortable, cold, quiet, noisy, beautiful
weather	hot, humid, cold
view	beautiful, spectacular

c Encourage students to ask and answer questions. This is not very communicative as the questions are practised not because the answers are interesting, but so that students get used to which adjectives can describe which nouns. The next part of the task **3d** *is* communicative.

d Set up the task. Ask one good student in your class:

Where did you spend your holiday last year? – In Tuscany.
Then ask: What was the hotel like? / What were the people like?
If the student didn't go away on holiday last year, ask about their last holiday.

Point out that it is not necessary to answer in whole sentences. One word answers are OK. Indeed it is more *natural* to answer in this way.

Make sure that students stand up and move about the classroom when they ask and answer the questions, otherwise they will only have answers from the two people who normally sit next to them. Use your discretion as to how many people you feel it is appropriate for the students to ask. More than five is probably too many. This gives students intensive practice in using the question form of the verb 'to be' in the past tense.

Have a report back session. Here the students have practice using the positive form of the verb 'to be' in the past tense.

4 The postcard

Aims
– to introduce all forms of the regular past tenses
– to give students practice in reading for information

a Considerable work has already been done on the question form but in the present tense (unit 3). This work will, however, mean that students should know what sort of answer is required for each question. A question with 'when' signifies the need for an answer with 'time' etc.

Key 4a

How did they get from the airport to the hotel? –
By car, by limousine.
Where did they relax for the first two days? –
By the swimming pool.
What did they do on Tuesday? –
They walked round/visited the markets.
When did they watch the laser show? –
At eight o'clock in the evening.

Ask students to read for the answers to the questions first.

Discourage them from just quoting whole chunks from the text: So, for example in the first question 'by limousine' is sufficient and is, in fact, a better answer than 'A courtesy limousine picked us up from the airport.'

b Draw attention to the form of both questions and answers.

All questions are formed with 'did + the infinitive'. Point out that 'did' is already the past tense and you don't need two such tenses in the questions (wrong example Did they relaxed).
Most regular verbs add -ed to form the past tense, but of course verbs that already end in 'e' simply add '-d', e.g. hope – hoped, decide – decided.
Verbs ending in one stressed vowel and one consonant double the consonant before adding -ed, e.g. shop – shopped, plan – planned.
Verbs ending in consonant + y, change y to i and add -ed, e.g. cry – cried, hurry – hurried.

There is a lot of information here and it is probably too much for students to absorb all at once. Concentrate on adding -d or -ed at first and then draw attention to other points as they arise.

Key 4b

did
-ed
I didn't believe it … / I didn't buy any …

When you have done this you can, if necessary, clarify any other vocabulary that students are still unsure of. They may need the reassurance but you should not clarify every word *before* they do the reading task. You want to discourage them from stopping at every word that they don't understand and encourage them to read for specific information.

5 Over to you

Aims
– to personalise the grammar
– to give students a reason to talk using both question and positive forms of the past
– to reinforce the question forms in the past tense

a Give some examples for yourself so that students know what information they have to write. They can either fill in the information on page 62 or they can write all the information on a piece of paper. The latter method might appeal to better students as they are not so restricted in what they can write. For example: On my last holiday I stayed with my family in a hotel near Dresden for three days. We travelled by train and the journey was long and boring. When I'm on holiday I like to try the local food. One evening we had a very expensive meal. The restaurant was …

Give students time to write their own text. Don't be frightened of silence here. Your students will be working hard but not necessarily talking! Be on hand to help with vocabulary if necessary.

b Then draw attention to the questions. This reinforces the 'Did +infinitive' construction for the formation of questions in the past.

Refer back to *your* holiday meal and encourage students to express sympathy or enthusiasm. You could also drill the students with appropriate responses, e.g.
The restaurant was by the harbour.
We waited an hour for the bill.
We didn't like the wine because it wasn't cold.
We didn't enjoy the food because it was cold.
It was still hot in the evening so we ate outside.
There was a good view from the restaurant.

Ask students to tell their partner about their holiday meal.

Now that students have seen and heard a variety of verbs in the past tense some work with the pronunciation of the past tense is useful. Although they all end in -ed, the pronunciation of this is not always the same.

Put three columns on the board: [t], [d] and [ɪd].

Read each of the following verbs and ask the students to categorise them in the right column: arrived, picked, travelled, relaxed, walked, shaved, watched, rested, stayed, posted, finished, started, paid, liked, ordered, wanted, enjoyed, ended, polished, decided, shout, served.

[t]	[d]	[ɪd]
polished	arrived	started
picked	travelled	wanted
relaxed	stayed	ended
walked	paid	shouted
watched	ordered	rested
finished	served	posted
liked	shaved	

Try to elicit some rules for pronunciation from the students.

The past ending -ed is pronounced as follows:
[d] after vowels and voiced consonants [ð], [b], [v], [z], [ʒ], [dʒ], [g], [m], [n], [ŋ], [l]

[t] after unvoiced consonants [θ], [p], [f], [s], [ʃ], [tʃ], [k]

[ɪd] after [d] and [t]

Refer students to exercises **1** and **2** in the **back-up section** on page 64 for more practice with the regular past tense.

Extra activity
Happy families
As pointed out in **4b** above there are a lot of spelling rules associated with the formation of the simple past tense. Students need a lot of practice before it can be said that they 'know' all these.

Procedure
1. Photocopy the happy family cards on the **worksheets on pages 66–67**. One set per group of three or four students. (You can't play this game with only two students.)
2. Cut them up.
3. Give each group a set of cards. Students shuffle them and then deal them to all the players in the group.
4. The aim of the game is to collect a set (a family) of four cards, all cards having *the same verb* in them.
5. Students look at their cards and see if they have any of the same set.
Then the game begins.

The first student looks at his incomplete sets of cards and decides which set he/she wants to complete first. The 'missing' sentences are written in small script on the cards. He or she then asks one student in the group for one of the missing cards. 'Have you got the sentence: He cried when his son was born?' If the player asked has indeed got the card, he or she must hand it over. If not, the answer is 'Sorry, I haven't' and that player then has a turn. The winner is the person who has the most sets of cards at the end of the game.

6 Your reservation

Aims
– to familiarise students with a typical on-line booking form for a hotel
– to give them practice in selective reading

What sort of room can you book in a hotel? –
A single, a double, a twin, a family room (A double bed and a single one).
What's the difference between a twin room and a double room? – Both for two people, but the room has either one bed or two.

Clarify the word 'inherited' (Someone dies and leaves you some money. You inherit it.).
Explain that he chose two possible dates for his short holiday, 10th-12th August or 28th-30th.
Ask students to look at the booking details and to answer the 'true/false/possible' questions.

Key 6b

1. false   For two nights.
2. true
3. false   They *left* on this date.
4. possible   It was full on the 10th and 11th and maybe also on the 12th but we don't *know*.
5. false   One big double bed, a King-sized bed (You can also have a Queen-sized bed that is a bit smaller!)
6. false   It was in a quiet location.
7. possible   There were facilities in the hotel, but maybe they didn't use them.
8. false   He paid £650 for the room for two nights.
9. possible
10. false   They probably travelled home after breakfast on the 30th.

Back-up section

Reference has been made throughout the unit as to the appropriate back-up exercises.
Exercise 3 can be prepared at home and then can form a warmer in the following lesson if this seems appropriate.

Reference to revision unit

If your students need some more speaking practice about holidays and some more work with comparison of adjectives, look at the revision unit on page 74.

Photocopiable worksheet for unit 6, warmer

	a shirt		a suit
	a skirt		a dress
	a tie		a swimming costume
	a pair of socks		a pair of jeans
	a pair of tights		a pair of gloves

Photocopiable worksheet for unit 6, extra activity (after 2)

Look at this list of features of a hotel. Add two of your own.
Which five features are important to you in a (holiday) hotel?

cheap ☐
clean ☐
quiet ☐
good food ☐
entertainment for the children ☐
entertainment in the evening ☐
sports facilities ☐
a fitness centre ☐
friendly service ☐
_____ ☐
_____ ☐

Look at this list of features of a hotel. Add two of your own.
Which five features are important to you in a (holiday) hotel?

cheap ☐
clean ☐
quiet ☐
good food ☐
entertainment for the children ☐
entertainment in the evening ☐
sports facilities ☐
a fitness centre ☐
friendly service ☐
_____ ☐
_____ ☐

Photocopiable worksheet for unit 6, extra activity (after 5)

She shopped in the department store. He shopped in the sports shop. They shopped on-line. We shopped at the car showroom.	**He shopped in the sports shop.** She shopped in the department store. They shopped on-line. We shopped at the car showroom.	**They shopped on-line.** We shopped at the car showroom. He shopped in the sports shop. She shopped in the department store.	**We shopped at the car showroom.** She shopped at the department store. He shopped in the sports shop. They shopped on-line.
We planned a party. They planned their holiday. She planned her business trip to Milan. He planned an important meeting.	**They planned their holiday.** She planned her business trip to Milan. He planned an important meeting. We planned a party.	**She planned her business trip to Milan.** He planned an important meeting. We planned a party. They planned their holiday.	**He planned an important meeting.** We planned a party. They planned their holiday. She planned her business trip to Milan.
She jogged for half an hour. We jogged round Central Park. He jogged ten kilometres. They jogged along the river.	**We jogged round Central Park.** He jogged ten kilometres. They jogged along the river. She jogged for half an hour.	**He jogged ten kilometres** They jogged along the river. She jogged for half an hour. We jogged round Central Park.	**They jogged along the river.** She jogged for half an hour. We jogged round Central park. He jogged ten kilometres.
We preferred to eat in the hotel. They preferred to eat in the Chinese restaurant. He preferred to eat a salad. She preferred to eat a sandwich at her desk.	**They preferred to eat in the Chinese restaurant.** He preferred to eat a salad. She preferred to eat a sandwich at her desk. We preferred to eat in the hotel.	**He preferred to eat a salad.** She preferred to eat a sandwich at her desk. We preferred to eat in the hotel. They preferred to eat in a Chinese restaurant.	**She preferred to eat a sandwich at her desk.** We preferred to eat in the hotel. They preferred to eat in the Chinese restaurant. He preferred to eat a salad.

Photocopiable worksheet for unit 6, extra activity (after 5)

She worried about her interview. He worried about his examination. They worried about their children. We worried about the long flight.	**He worried about his examination.** They worried about their children. We worried about the long flight. She worried about her interview.	**They worried about their children.** We worried about the long flight. She worried about her interview. He worried about his examination.	**We worried about the long flight.** She worried about her interview. He worried about his examination. They worried about their children.
They hurried to catch the bus. She hurried to catch her plane. He hurried to meet his children from school. We hurried to welcome our guests.	**She hurried to catch her plane.** He hurried to meet his children from school. We hurried to welcome our guests. They hurried to catch the bus.	**He hurried to meet his children from school.** We hurried to welcome our guests. They hurried to catch the bus. She hurried to catch her plane.	**We hurried to welcome our guests.** They hurried to catch the bus. She hurried to catch her plane. He hurried to meet his children from school.
They tried to lose weight. We tried to book a hotel room. He tried to learn Chinese. She tried to phone him.	**We tried to book a hotel room.** He tried to learn Chinese. She tried to phone him. They tried to lose weight.	**He tried to learn Chinese.** She tried to phone him. They tried to lose weight. We tried to book a hotel room.	**She tried to phone him.** They tried to lose weight. We tried to book a hotel room. He tried to learn Chinese.
She cried because she was happy. He cried when his son was born. They cried at the wedding. We cried because the film was sad.	**He cried when his son was born.** They cried at the wedding. We cried because the film was sad. She cried because she was happy.	**They cried at the wedding.** We cried because the film was sad. She cried because she was happy. He cried when his son was born.	**We cried because the film was sad.** She cried because she was happy. He cried when his son was born. They cried at the wedding.

© 2005 Max Hueber Verlag
This sheet may be photocopied and used within the class.

UNIT 7   Too much waste?

Topics:	Recycling and how to avoid waste.
Vocabulary:	dumpster diving; charities; recycling
Structures:	past simple of irregular verbs, positive and negative; imperatives (positive and negative); if sentences type 1
Functions:	expressing dos and don'ts; requesting politely
Skills:	listening for detail (in a text about dumpster diving); listening for gist; reading to understand text structure
Pronunciation:	sentence stress used to correct information
Job Talk:	polite requests
Culture corner:	British and American English; charities
Learning tip:	learning irregular verbs; how to practise pronunciation
Reading for fun:	Text number 9: The Teddy bear
Time considerations:	lesson 1: 1 and 2 (with a good group also 3)
	lesson 2: (3), 4, 5, 6 (5 could be omitted if time is short)
	lesson 3: 7, 8 (with a weak group work on reading skills (8) will take a whole lesson)

Warmer

Guess the number.
Write the following on the board: 190, 290, 590, 88, 12.
This tells you about the number of litres of water an average person uses every day in the following countries: Germany, Mali, USA, France, China. Which is which?

Answers:
Germany   190
France   290
USA   590
China   88
Mali   12

1 Recycle it

Aims
– to introduce the topic of waste
– to introduce the past simple of irregular verbs in the positive form
– to give students practice in listening for gist and for detail

a The warmer leads on to the topic of waste. How do we waste water?
So do you agree with the statement in **1a**?

Point out that 'dumpster' is an American word. The British English is a 'skip'.

This listening text is the longest in the book so far and there needs to be careful preparation so that learners get the most out of it.

First look at the picture of the person in the dumpster: Ask students to speculate as to what the person is doing. Is it a he or a she do you think? Why is (s)he looking in the dumpster? (S)he has lost something, (s)he is looking to see what (s)he can find and sell or use again.

b Then look at the sentences a-g. You could ask students what sort of words they might hear when they listen for the answers in a.-g.

Some suggestions might be:
a. bored, new hobby, boyfriend did it and she wanted to be with him, friends liked it

b. bed, chair, table, TV
c. What would she do with the clothes? Wear them? Give them away? If so, give them to who?
d. She helps people? It's certainly different.
e. Food that has passed its sell-by date; old bread, old vegetables, tins that are a strange shape?
f. Toy animals. What would she do with them when she'd found them? Wash and repair them?
g. Three have been mentioned already.

Then play the text and stop it where indicated by a line ____ so that students can decide what the paragraph is about and fill in the appropriate number.

Tapescripts 1b / Track 26 / Key

Interviewer: Welcome to our environmental series "Don't Throw It Away". This week I am talking to Heather Steele who is a dumpster diver. Someone who searches other people's garbage to see what they can find and recycle. So – how did you first become a dumpster diver Heather?
Heather: I read about this hobby on a web-site. I didn't have an exciting hobby and I thought it sounded fun and interesting.
____ **Why she became a dumpster diver: a1**

Interviewer: So what did you do then?
Heather: Well, before I began I went to the library to check that it was legal. I didn't want to have any problems with law enforcement officers. My husband's dad is a cop!
Interviewer: So what then?
Heather: Well, I was very nervous about my first dumpster dive but it was no problem. I didn't plan to do it. I was in a supermarket car park. I was by my car and a man came out with a cart full of bottles of orange juice and threw them away. I saw the juice was still OK so I took ten bottles out of the dumpster and put them into the trunk of my car.
____ **The supermarket dumpster dive : e2**

Interviewer: So when was that?
Heather: That was three years ago and I am now a real enthusiast and know where to go to get the best results.

Interviewer: So where do you go dumpster diving?
Heather: My three favourite dumpsters are at the back of an apartment block, next to a furniture store and by a toy store.
____ **Her three favourite dumpsters: g3**

Interviewer: Why there?
Heather: Well, people from the apartment block move quite often and you know what it's like when you move. You throw things away. At this block people throw away clothes mostly. I sent about 4,000 items of clothing to a hostel for homeless people last year and all from one dumpster!
____ **The dumpster behind the apartment block: c4**

Interviewer: Wow! Do you always give things away that you find in the dumpsters?
Heather: Not always. Two weeks ago I found a TV in the furniture store dumpster and my husband repaired it and we gave it to our daughter.
____ **The furniture store dumpster : b5**

Interviewer: What is the best thing you found so far?
Heather: That's easy. Twenty soft toy animals. They were at the bottom of the toy store dumpster and were dirty and had ears or eyes missing, but we washed and repaired them and spent a wonderful day at a children's home where we gave each kid a toy for Christmas.
____ **The toy store dumpster: f6**

Interviewer: So a worthwhile hobby, but isn't it a dirty one?
Heather: Not at all. A lot of sports are much dirtier than dumpster diving. It's like a treasure hunt. I think it is a wonderful way to recycle and have fun. Why don't you try it!
____ **Why she likes the hobby: d7**

Interviewer: Maybe I will.

7

c Then play it again for more detailed comprehension. Again you will need to stop the CD when students have heard each piece of information so that they have the time to fill in the answers in **1c**.

Key 1c

1. on a web-site
2. the library
3. bottles of orange juice
4. three years ago
5. 4,000
6. TV / daughter
7. 20 soft toy animals
8. a children's home

d There is a list of the most common irregular verbs on page 133.

Key 1d

begin/began, find/found, give/gave, go/went, read/read, send/sent, spend/spent, take/took, put/put

2 Are you a good detective?

Aim
– to give students practice in using the past simple of irregular verbs in the positive form

a Let the students look at the pictures and decide what the person did as in the example.

Suggestions:
flew from Philadelphia to New Orleans; went on a tour of the Bayou; went to Williamsburg; went to a Cajun restaurant; ate some liquorice all sorts, some pretzel pieces, some pretzels, some donuts, some chocolate, some chocolate almonds, some soup; drank some wine

Do they think this is a man or a woman? They might also say the person eats a lot of sweet things that are not very good for them!

Background information
A 'bayou' is 'a swampy arm or slow-moving outlet of a lake'. The term is mainly used in Mississippi or Louisiana. A feature of these wetlands is the cypress trees and such areas also have an abundance of wildlife including alligators, snakes, egrets, herons.

Cajun cooking
'Cajuns' (or Acadians) found a new home in South Louisiana after being exiled from their initial homeland in France and having to move from place to place. This history of being always on the move meant that they were adaptable and this was reflected in their cuisine. They made no attempt to recreate the classical cuisine of Europe. They lived off the land using fish, shellfish and wild game. Ingredients were carefully combined in the black iron pots of the Cajuns into one pot meals. Today, stews, fricassees, soups, spicy sausages, gumbos (dishes made from the okra plant), piquant sauces and stuffed vegetables are all characteristic of the Cajun cuisine.

b You may like to 'sanitise' your wallet/handbag/pocket for this activity. Show the students the contents for them to guess what you did last week. Insist on the correct past tense in the answers.

c Then ask students to work in pairs and show each other the contents of their wallet/handbag/pocket so that they can reconstruct what they did last week.

Draw students' attention to the **learning tip** at the bottom of page 67 and the list of irregular verbs on page 133.

3 That's not right

Aims
– to introduce the negative of irregular past tenses
– to focus on voice pitch when correcting information
– to consolidate vocabulary from the listening text

a Focus on the example sentence and the form of the negative. Point out that 'Didn't' is already in the past so we don't need two parts of the verb in the past. Allow students to look at the tapescript on page 137 and come up with the answers. Check in plenary.

b Refer back to the example sentence and the words underlined. These are stressed and so the pitch of the voice goes up. Explain that the students should listen to the five sentences and decide which words are stressed and write them down.

Get students to repeat the sentences. Give everyone a chance to say at least one, even if this will mean repeating some sentences. Students often find *hearing* the change in pitch difficult and so the more practice they get the better. Hence the learning tip.

Tapescripts 3b / Track 27

(key for 3a and 3b underlined words)
1. She didn't begin it <u>four years ago</u>, she began <u>three years ago</u>.
2. She didn't give it to a <u>children's home</u>, she gave it to their daughter.
3. She didn't send <u>5,000</u> items, she sent <u>4,000</u>.
4. She didn't read about it in a <u>newspaper</u>, she read about it on a <u>web-site</u>.
5. They didn't take them to a <u>school</u>, they took them to a <u>children's home</u>.

Refer student to exercises and **2** and **4** in the **back-up section** for practice with the past tense and voice pitch.

4 Five verbs and five questions

Aims
– to give students practice in the question form in the past tense
– to encourage students to share information about themselves

Give an example yourself. Write two verbs in the past tense on the board and encourage students to find out why you wrote them using the question form in the past tense.
So the prompt 'buy' might encourage the questions: Did you buy a new car? Did you buy some new clothes? Did you buy a present for your partner?
You should reply with 'Yes, I did.' or 'No, I didn't.' as appropriate.

Then ask students to write down five verbs on five pieces of paper. They then work with a partner and show these to him or her, one at a time. The partner has to guess why they were written by asking questions.

Have a feedback session when students share one thing their partner did last week.

5 British or American?

Aims
– to focus on the differences in vocabulary in British and American English
– to have fun learning vocabulary

The basis for the book *English Elements – Refresher A2* is British English. Spelling is British English (so, for example: colour *not* color, advertise *not* advertize) However, it should be pointed out that there are many varieties of English, all correct, just different. The aim of the **learning tip** is to encourage students to notice these differences if they are on holiday in USA, Australia, New Zealand, South Africa or indeed anywhere else where notices in hotels and restaurants are in English.

First check that students know the British English words for the American ones in the examples.
garbage – rubbish
trunk – boot
store – shop
apartment block – block of flats

Divide students into pairs. You can use the **photocopiable activity on page 75**. Copy and cut up the same number of names of cities as you have students. Give each student the name of a city at random. Students have to find their partner by finding the European and American city with the same letter. So: Miami and Milan.
If you have an uneven number of students, make sure you include Paris so that you have a group of three: Philadelphia, Prague and Paris.

When students have found their partner allocate letter A or B to each student. If you have an odd number, two students will have to have the same letter.

Direct students A to page 112 and students B to page 115. Explain that they first have to guess what the 'translations' of the words are in either British or American English and then they should compare with their partner.

UNIT 7   71

Key 5

petrol	gas
lift	elevator
bill	check
torch	flashlight
tap	faucet
handbag	purse
taxi	cab
underground	subway
film	movie
motorway	highway
mobile phone	cell phone
rubber	eraser

If you have a relaxed relationship with your class you might like to point out the embarrassing situation that might arise if the word 'rubber' is used in American English. This means condom! Also point out that the words 'subway' and 'purse' are both used in British English but they have different meanings.
subway – an underpass for pedestrians under a busy road
purse – something you keep your money in

If you want to practise the vocabulary again, you can do the following anagram activity.
Copy the **photocopiable worksheet on page 76** onto an overhead transparency.

Procedure
The class works in two teams.
Reveal the anagrams one at a time and the first team to guess the word gets a point. Then the *other* team has to give the 'translation' of that word. The team with the most points wins.

Key

taxi, trunk, subway, store, tap, lift, elevator, motorway, underground, purse, movie, eraser

6 Can you lend it to me?

Aim
– to give students practice in making and responding to polite requests

First ask students to think of the things from **5** that *could* have been left in the hotel room. They are going to hear dialogues when someone has left something in the hotel. Not *all* the objects forgotten are from activity **5**. Then play the CD and ask students to complete **6a** with the objects that have been forgotten.

Tapescripts 6a / Track 28

(key for 6a and 6b, words underlined)

1. ▲ Look, Ian, I left my <u>mobile</u> in my hotel room. <u>Could you</u> phone a taxi for me at about four thirty?
   ● <u>Sure.</u>
   ▲ Thanks.

2. ▲ Hi, Jane. An emergency. I left my <u>purse</u> in the hotel room. <u>Could you possibly</u> lend me £15 to pay the taxi?
   ● <u>Of course.</u> Let me see …OK. Here you are.
   ▲ Thanks a lot. You saved my life.

3. ▲ Hello, John. Look, I left my <u>laser pointer</u> in my hotel room. <u>Could you</u> lend me one, just for this morning?
   ● <u>Sorry</u>, I need it this morning. Why don't you ask Peter.
   ▲ OK. Thanks.

4. ▲ Morning Julia.
   ● Hi.
   ▲ Look, I left my <u>stapler</u> in the hotel room this morning. <u>Could you</u> staple these papers for me?
   ● <u>I'm sorry, but</u> my stapler doesn't work. Ask Judith. She can do it for you.
   ▲ Thanks.

Check the answers and then play the CD a second time, focussing on the way to make a polite request and respond.

UNIT 7

Request
Could you ...?
Could you possibly ...?

Positive answer
Sure.
Of course.

Negative answer
I'm sorry ...
I'm sorry but ...

Try to elicit why the request for the £15 is 'Could you possibly ...?' rather than simply 'Could you ...?' When you are asking quite a big favour (for money!) then you have to be more polite and this politeness is signified by the inclusion of the word 'possibly'. It is also possible to ask 'Can you ...?' for a polite request. 'Could you ...?' has been used here as it is more appropriate in a business situation where extra politeness is important.

Now let students work in pairs to practise the dialogues on page 138. Before they start use the picture to help with ideas for some more requests, ones that were not on the CD (for example, 'Could I use your phone?').

Refer students to exercise 3 in the **back-up section** that practises requests.

7 Rules

Aims
– to introduce and practise the use of imperatives
– to introduce the first conditional to talk about possible situations that may happen

a, b Refer back to the dumpster diver text. Just like for an hobby there are rules. Encourage students to match the two halves of the rules and then to compare ideas with a partner before you play the CD to check.

Tapescripts 7b / Track 29

(key for 7a, words underlined)

Bill: Welcome to the phone-in program about dumpster diving. Our first caller is Karen. So what's your question, Karen?

Karen: Hi, Bill. I'm new to this hobby. I went to the police and asked about it. It is legal in our area but are there any other things I should think about?

Bill: Hi, Karen. Well, it's good to know that it's legal in your area but don't climb over a fence to reach a dumpster and remember it's a hobby for people who care about waste and the environment, so don't take more than you need, leave the area cleaner than you found it and don't make a lot of noise.

Karen: OK. You mentioned leave the area tidy. Do you get dirty dumpster diving?

Bill: Well, not if you are careful. Wear gloves, wash your hands when you finish and, er, don't forget a first aid kit.

Karen: Thanks a lot.

Bill: No problem. Have fun.

Then, if necessary, focus on the form of the commands.
Allow students to work in groups. Give them these two situations: 'in a car' and 'in a plane'. Ask them to think of as many commands as possible that are appropriate in that situation.

In a car: wear a seat belt, don't drive too fast, don't blow your horn near a hospital, take the car for a check-up regularly, don't drink and drive, stop at a red light, don't drive over a red light.

In a plane: don't smoke, don't use a mobile phone, don't use a computer on take-off and landing, keep your seat belt fastened, put your hand luggage under your seat, be careful when you open the overhead locker.

c Now bring the topic back to the environment. Put the following command on the right side of the board as in the example: ... don't leave the tap running when you clean your teeth.

Why is this a bad idea for the environment? Because you use a lot of water and we want to save water. When we talk about something that must happen before something else happens, we talk about a condition. We have to *want* to save water first before we think about not leaving the tap on. In conditional clauses we use the little word "if". So to complete our sentence (at this point write in the left-hand column):

If you want to save water, ...

One sort of conditional clause is formed with the present tense in the 'if'-clause and commands in the main clause. Refer to the grammar box on page 70. Then look at the other conditional clauses: What must happen if we want to save trees?
Elicit a few ideas to clarify what needs to be done and then allow students to work with a partner to think of as many possible endings to the sentence stems as possible. Have a feedback session so that ideas can be shared.

Refer students to exercise **1** on page 72 in the **back-up section** for more work with commands and conditional sentences.

8 Don't throw it away, recycle it!

Aims
- to give students practice in reading for detail
- to give students practice in reading to understand the organisation of a text
- to activate students' knowledge of the world that will help in the comprehension process

a Talk about the questions in **8a**. You could add: Why might a car fail its inspection?

Pre-text activity
Copy the **photocopiable worksheet on page 77**. You will need to copy half as many worksheets as you have students in the class. Cut the worksheet in half, into columns A and B.

Procedure
1. Divide your class in half and give half the class words from column A and half the class words from column B.
2. Tell them they are going to read a text with their words in it. What do they think the text will be about? Students should discuss this.
3. Have some feedback from the two halves of the class.

Then tell the class they are going to read a text with *all* the words in it. What do they think the text will be about now?

b Then look at the text. Remind the students that 'cop' is the American for 'policeman'. Look at the title and predict what the story will be about.

Then allow the students to read the first paragraph (c) to themselves. Give them the questions to answer:

What happened to his car?
Why did he want to say goodbye to his car?
Check they understand it.

Then you want to guide the students as to how they find out what the next paragraph is. Explain that there is usually a link between paragraphs.
Read the last sentence: It sounded interesting. What does 'it' refer to?
So to find the next paragraph they need to find something to do with charity.
Then let them do the whole activity and re-order the paragraphs.

Give a time limit for this as the idea's not to read for detailed understanding at this stage. Five minutes with a good group. Make sure students understand they are not meant to read all the text at the moment, they are meant to find the order of the paragraphs.

Key 8b

1c, 2b, 3e, 4d, 5a, 6f

Ask the students what the 'clues' were, what links they found.

paragraph 1-2	This charity.
paragraph 2-3	money
paragraph 3-4	in shock
paragraph 4-5	'traffic patrolman' and 'on patrol'
paragraph 5-6	I knew then (when I read about the traffic patrolman)

c Then students can read the text more slowly to answer the 'true/false' questions at the bottom of the page.

Key 8c

1. false (rust)
2. false (people from the charity)
3. false (he got a tax reduction)
4. true
5. true
6. false (the driver screamed and shouted at the patrolman)

Then ask about charities that students give money to.

Back-up section

Reference has been made to the appropriate exercises throughout the unit.

Exercise **5** on vocabulary is one that can be usefully done in class time. Recognising word stress is an important skill for students to learn so that they can use a dictionary sensibly. The system of dots has been adopted here as it is very visual. Dictionaries mark stress in different ways and you should draw attention to this.

For example:
a'partment   (the most widely used method)
ap<u>art</u>ment
aPARTment

If students then meet a new word, you can write it on the board, marking stress in whichever way you feel is appropriate and ask *them* to make an attempt at pronouncing it. If they don't get it right at the first attempt, you can also make the stress clear by banging on the table: with the palm of your hand for the stressed syllable and with you knuckles for the unstressed ones.

Reference to revision unit

If your students need more work with the simple past, look at the speaking and reading activities on pages 76 and 77 of revision unit 2.

Photocopiable worksheet for unit 7, extra activity (for 5)

Miami	Milan
Washington	Warsaw
Boston	Budapest
Philadelphia	Prague
Chicago	Cambridge
Dallas	Dresden
San Francisco	Strasbourg
Las Vegas	Lausanne
New Orleans	Nuremberg
Kansas City	Klagenfurt
Paris	

© 2005 Max Hueber Verlag
This sheet may be photocopied and used within the class.

Photocopiable worksheet for unit 7, extra activity (for 5)

iatx
knutr
wabsyu
retos
apt
flit
vlateroe
yomotraw
drungruodne
resup
ovime
serare

Photocopiable worksheet for unit 7, extra activity (for 8)

List A	List B
on patrol	cry
ambulance driver	daughter
tax reduction	teddy bear
speeding ticket	shock
inspection	charity
spare parts	donation
repair	smile
dealer	trauma
highway	help

UNIT 8 What would you do?

Topics:	Food and health; speculating how you would react in certain situations.
Vocabulary:	adjectives to express feelings; rules and regulations; health problems
Structures:	if sentences type 2; modal verbs (should, mustn't, have to)
Functions:	complaining and apologising; explaining rules
Skills:	listening for gist; reading for gist (in chat room postings); selective reading (scanning to find food on a menu)
Pronunciation:	listening for the difference between the two sounds [ʃ] and [tʃ]
Job Talk:	pub lunches – responding to requests
Culture corner:	in a British pub
Learning tip:	categorising words according to sounds in your word bank
Reading for fun:	Text 10: Opening hours
Time considerations:	lesson 1: 1, 2
	lesson 2: 3, 4, 5 (4 and 5 will take a whole lesson with a weak class)
	lesson 3: 6, 7, 8, 9

1 Feelings

Aims
- to break the ice
- to introduce the idea of feelings
- to reinforce the -ing form used for what is happening now
- to introduce the second conditional used for speculating

a This first activity can serve as a warmer and lead-in to **1b**.
Ask students to look at the pictures and decide what emotions they represent.

Key 1a

1: tired, 2: sad, 3: happy, 4: bored, 5: angry, 6: cold

Then ask them how they are feeling. It can be useful for you to know who is feeling tired or sad in case they affect the group dynamics. Students may not always tell you, but if they trust you they will.

b Clarify some vocabulary before you ask students to complete this task, e.g. cough, litter, ignore, blow the horn.
Students should first decide which three people make them the angriest and then compare notes with a partner. Finally, ask the class as a whole which three people make them feel the angriest.

Then ask if they *do* something positive when they are angry or if they just kick the cat?!

c In this part of task 1 students' attention is focussed on 'would' in the main clause rather than the past tense in the 'if clause', as they have to respond to the four questions using 'Yes, I would' or 'No, I wouldn't'. Allow time for students to give their ideas using the prompts at the bottom of the page.

Then write one of the sentences from **1c** on the board and focus on the form of the verb in the 'if clause'. We use the past tense when we are imagining possible situations, but ones that are not real now.

The sentence 'If my car broke down, I'd use my mobile and phone my partner.' suggests that it is, of course, possible that the car will break down but it probably will not happen (It is a very expensive and reliable car, not an old and unreliable one!)

d This activity picks up the idea of what may happen but what we think will not and therefore the use of the second conditional. This task gives students the chance to choose the questions they want to ask. It also gives you, the teacher, a chance to check if students can form the second conditional correctly, so circulate when the students are writing their questions.

Refer students to exercise 1 in the **back-up section** which gives more practice in the use of the second conditional.

Key 1d

What would you do if ...?
- your car broke down on the motorway?
- you lost your voice?
- you locked yourself out of the house?
- you saw someone trying to steal a car?
- someone stole your handbag/wallet when you were on holiday?
- your family pet ran away?
- you needed a lot of money urgently?
- you broke your glasses / lost your contact lenses?

2 This is serious

Aims
- to give students practice in reading for gist
- to give further practice in the use of the second conditional
- to introduce the topic of food and healthy eating

a, b This task can be omitted if time is short, but it gives valuable practice in reading for gist and it forms a smooth link between the grammar point in **1** and the topic of healthy eating that follows in **3**.

Explain the notion of 'to go to court'. It is already common in the USA and increasingly so in the UK for individuals to sue, to take legal action if they have problems with goods and services. In hotel rooms, for example, you see notices such as 'Caution – hot water!', 'This towel rail can get hot!', 'Safety procedures when using the shower: always use the non-slip mat and don't use bath oils.' or 'Mind the step'. These notices make sure that the hotel *can't* be sued for not warning their customers of possible dangers. Remember the now infamous case when someone sued McDonald's because the coffee was hot.

Ask students to look at the headlines and predict what words are missing. Play the CD to check.

Key 2a

The missing word in the headlines is: fast food.

Tapescripts 2b / Track 33

The two teenagers from New York who took a big fast food chain to court lost their case today. The boys said they had health problems because they ate in the fast food restaurant and lawyers argued that the company didn't tell the truth about the contents of the food or warn their customers about the health risks. Food activists are saying that this case could be the beginning of a lot of legal problems for the multinational fast food companies.

Ask for reactions to this story.

c There are four chat room postings in all for this activity, one on page 80 and three in the **files section**. The reading material can be flexible to fit any size class as you can use a varying number of texts as appropriate.

If you have strong students in your class, simply divide them up into groups of three or four, depending on the numbers, and give each person in each group a different letter A, B, C or D and refer them to the appropriate text in the files section. Ask them to read their text and then share the essential information from it with the other members of their group.

If you have weaker students who might need help with comprehension, ask them to work in three or four groups (or pairs if you only have a small class). Give each pair or group a letter and they read the

8

appropriate chat room posting in the files section. As they read be on hand to help with vocabulary if necessary. In the next phase of this activity give each person in the group a number. Then ask students to work in a new group with people who have the same number as they do.

3 A healthy diet?

Aim
– to introduce and practise the modal auxiliaries 'should' and 'shouldn't'

a Refer back to the chat room postings. What positive and negative things did the people who visited the chat room have to say about fast food restaurants?

Then refer to the **grammar box** at the bottom of page 81 to focus on how to express what is a good idea to do and what is a bad idea to do. So what do doctors tell us is a good idea to do and what not to do? What do they say we should and shouldn't do?

Then look at the Mediterranean diet pyramid and ask students to answer the true/false questions, compare answers with a partner and then to check in plenary if this is necessary with a weak group.

Key 3a

1. True
2. False (you should)
3. True
4. False (every day)
5. False (you should eat it once a week)
6. True
7. True
8. True

b Then ask students, still in their pairs, to look at the pyramid and to come up with some more sentences with 'should' and 'shouldn't'. Do they take this advice? Do they eat meat once a month and fish once a week?

4 Doctors!

Aims
– to introduce and practise the modal auxiliary verbs 'mustn't', 'have to' and 'don't have to'
– to give further practice in the use of 'should' and 'shouldn't'

a The grammar topic of auxiliary verbs is a complicated one particularly with regard to 'must' and 'have to'. Both refer to necessity and obligation. 'Must' is used to give strong advice to ourselves (e.g. I must go to the dentist's. – I make the decision to go.) and to other people (e.g. Passengers must have a valid ticket. – The speaker has the authority). 'Have to' is used when the obligation comes from outside, from regulations (e.g. I have to take strong tablets for hay fever. – My doctor tells me to.). In American English 'have to' is preferred and indeed strong advice to ourselves is more and more often expressed by 'have to' in current British English.
There is the added confusion for German learners between 'mustn't' ('nicht dürfen, es ist verboten') and 'don't have to' ('nicht müssen').

So, at this low level, the decision has been made to restrict the modals to 'mustn't' and 'have to / don't have to'. The aim is to discourage students from using 'must' and encourage them to use 'have to'. If students ask about 'must', you can refer them to the note in the **grammar reference section** on page 131 where the distinction is made between what you *say* and what you *read*.

Before you begin with task **4** you may want to do some preparatory work on vocabulary. You will need to find a picture of a person modelling swimwear from a magazine. Show it to the class and ask students to tell you as many words for parts of the body as they remember. Make sure that 'ankle' and 'arm' are labelled as they come in the listening text. Then ask how a doctor might help you if you are ill.

Now play the CD and simply ask students to listen for the medical problem that each person has.

Tapescripts 4a / Track 34

(key underlined)

1. *Janet:* Haltwhistle 56921
   Roger: Hi, Janet. This is Roger.
   Janet: Roger! Nice to hear from you. How are you?
   Roger: Fine. Look, Janet, I'm sorry to bother you but could you do me a favour and give me a lift to the station? My car won't start.
   Janet: I'm sorry but <u>I've got a problem with my ankle</u> and <u>I mustn't walk on it</u>. <u>I have to use crutches.</u>
   Roger: Oh dear. I'm sorry to hear that. Is it painful?
   Janet: It's better than it was last week.
   Roger: Good. Get well soon.
   Janet: Thanks. Sorry I couldn't help.
   Roger: Never mind.

2. *Brian:* 6224586
   Jim: Brian?
   Brian: Speaking.
   Jim: Hi, Brian. I didn't recognise your voice. This is Jim. Would you like to come to the pub for a beer with Sam and me?
   Brian: Well, I'd love to, mate, <u>but I'm taking strong tablets for hay fever</u> at the moment so <u>I have to keep off the alcohol.</u>
   Jim: I don't believe it. You off the alcohol!
   Brian: 'Fraid so. <u>I mustn't drive</u> either. So life's no fun at the moment.
   Jim: Not for too long, though, eh?
   Brian: No, see ya around.
   Jim: Yeah, see ya.

3. *Anita:* Watford Library. Can I help you?
   Sally: Anita?
   Anita: Yeah?
   Sally: Hi, Anita. This is Sally. Look would you like to come shopping after work?
   Anita: Normally I'd love to, but <u>I've got problems with my arm</u> and <u>I have to keep it in a sling</u>.
   Sally: Oh dear. And I suppose you certainly <u>mustn't carry heavy shopping bags</u>!
   Anita: You guessed it.
   Sally: Does your arm hurt?
   Anita: Not much. It's just annoying.
   Sally: Oh, well, another time. Get well soon. Bye.
   Anita: Bye for now.

Check the answers and clarify 'hay fever' and 'sling'.

So when you are ill you go to the doctor's and he or she tells you what is 100% necessary to do (e.g. Take these tablets, stay in bed, take this medicine) and what is forbidden to do (e.g. Don't drive a car when you take this medicine, don't go to work next week.).

So the patient has instructions from the doctor. Now listen again for what the patient 'has to do' and what the patient 'mustn't' do.

Play the CD again and check the answers.

Focus on the **grammar box** on page 82 to make the distinction between 'have to' and 'mustn't'.

Students will need a lot of practice with these new structures. There is a **photocopiable worksheet on page 87** that can give them some practice in recognising the difference in meaning between 'have to' and 'mustn't'.

Procedure

1. Make enough copies of the worksheet so that each pair has one copy.
2. Cut up the two halves of the sentences.
3. Give them to the students who are working in pairs.
4. The students have to reassemble the sentences.

Key to extra activity

She has to take medicine three times a day.
They have to eat a lot of vegetables to stay healthy.
She has to walk with crutches.
He has to go to the dentist's regularly because he has got very bad teeth.
You mustn't eat sweets if you want to have good teeth.
You mustn't go to work today because you've got a temperature.
I have to take these tablets after meals.
I mustn't eat salmon because I have a fish allergy.
She mustn't drive when she is taking the tablets.
She has to go to the doctor's regularly because she is pregnant.

You could then extend the activity by asking students to complete some or all of the sentence stems in their own way. You may need to prompt them and you may need to help with vocabulary. It

8

is, however, good to allow students say what *they* want to. This activity will be a good indicator as to whether the students understand the meaning of 'mustn't' or whether they are confusing it with the German 'nicht müssen'.

She has to take	– her children to school every morning.
	– tablets for blood pressure.
They have to eat	– spinach because it is good for them.
	– oranges because they have vitamin C.
She has to walk	– five miles to school.
	– ten miles every day.
You mustn't eat	– too much chocolate if you want to lose weight.
	– sweets before supper.
You mustn't go to work	– if you are ill.
I have to	– pay for ...
	– work ... hours a week.
I mustn't eat	– ... because I am allergic to it.
She mustn't drive	– a car because her eyes are very weak.
	– at night because her eyes are weak.
She has to go to the doctor's regularly	– because she has high blood pressure.
	– she has a bad heart.
	– she takes a lot of tablets and she needs a prescription.

b Now refer students back to the tapescript. The friends were ill, but they are now OK. There are no problems. It is not necessary for Janet to walk with crutches, it is not necessary for Brian to take tablets for his hay fever, it is not necessary for Anita to keep her arm in a sling. Refer to the **grammar box** on page 82. Then you could adapt the sentences from the **photocopiable worksheet** mentioned above to include the new structure:

I don't have to eat	spinach if I don't like it.
I don't have to go to the doctor's regularly	because I am very healthy.
He doesn't have to go to work	at the weekend, on Saturdays or on a public holiday.

5 Come to Utopia!

Aim
– to bring together all the modals covered so far in the unit and to give students practice in their use

a Ask students what, for them, would be Utopia. Give an example to stimulate their imaginations: For me, Utopia is where you don't have to get up early, you don't have to eat spinach etc.

Explain that the country described in **5** on page 82 is Utopia for families and animal lovers. Students then make sensible sentences from the table taking one element from each column.

The sentences that students come up with will depend on their point of view. This is part of the fun. So if they are cyclists, but hate wearing hats one of their sentences may be:
Cyclists don't have to wear crash hats. Allow them to make up their own sentences and then share them with the class.

Possible sentences:

cyclists	should wear crash hats; have to wear crash hats; mustn't ride on the pavement; should be careful of pedestrians
children	should/don't have to eat healthy food; should/don't have to/mustn't!!! help their parents with the washing up; mustn't ride on the pavement
car drivers	should be careful of pedestrians; have to slow down near schools
dog owners	have to/don't have to keep their dog on a lead
parents	have to/should give their children a lot of pocket money; don't have to pay for hospital treatment; don't have to eat healthy food

b This task gives students the opportunity to make up their own sentences with the modal verbs. When they have written their ten sentences have a feedback session and the listeners can decide whether they would like to live in these countries.

Refer students to exercise **2** in the **back-up section** where there is more work with these modal verbs.

6 Sunday lunch

Aims
- to give students practice in selective reading (scanning)
- to increase students' vocabulary in the lexical field of food

a First brainstorm food. Have word wheels on the board for meat and fish, fruit and vegetables and groceries so that students are encouraged to categorise words, so making them easier to learn.

Don't overdo the vocabulary load here. Students may ask for a lot of new words, but more can sometimes be less. The idea is to re-activate forgotten vocabulary rather than to introduce twenty or thirty new lexical items. Make sure that 'lettuce' is included (point out that this is the translation for 'grüner Salat' in German) and also 'garlic' as students at this level may not know it and it is needed so that students can complete the next task.

b The menu on page 84 is a real one from a pub in Yorkshire and is typical of menus in many pubs run by a restaurant chain. Language is quite flowery. Potatoes are never just 'potatoes', but are 'glazed Charlotte potatoes'. Peas are never 'peas' but 'fresh green garden peas'. The idea of this task is for students to ignore all the flowery words that they don't know and to focus on the words for food that they *do* know. Set a time limit of five minutes for this task as the idea is to scan the menu on page 84 quickly to find the answers to the questions rather than to understand every word.

Key 6b

2 sorts of cheese:	Brie, parmesan
2 sorts of fish:	salmon, sea bass (they won't know 'Bass' but should be able to guess because of 'sea'; students may say 'crab' which is officially a shell fish)
4 sorts of vegetables:	tomato, potato, mushroom, peppers
something hot / for a curry:	chilli, coriander, spices
something yellow:	lemon, mayonnaise
something that smells:	garlic

c Check this and then ask students to read the menu again and to decide who from the list in 6c would choose which food.

Key 6c

Bob	tomato soup
Janie	roast Norfolk turkey
Andrew	roast nut, mushroom and spinach loaf
Wendy	crab and salmon fish cake
Lee	tomato soup, sirloin of beef

Background information
If participants ask about Bloomer bread, Charlotte potatoes etc. the following information may be of interest.

A. sea bass: 'Barsch' in German
B. Norfolk turkey: Norfolk is a county in England where the turkey came from
C. Victoria plum: is a type of plum; it is like saying 'golden delicious' for an apple
D. Bloomer bread:

Ingredients
1-1/2 cups unbleached flour
2-1/4 cups whole wheat flour
1 teaspoon. salt
1 tablespoons. wheat germ
1/2 teaspoon. dry yeast
1-1/2 cups warm milk

Preparation
Mix the dry ingredients, except for the yeast, in a large bowl. Mix together the yeast with the warm water or milk. Add to the dry ingredients, mix well, then knead the dough until smooth and elastic (between 6 and 8 minutes). Roll the dough in flour, put it in a warm bowl and leave at room temperature 3-4 hours. Then flatten it and knead it again, roll in flour and let rise again, about another 2-3 hours. Flatten the dough again and then give it a final kneading, shape into a fat baguette shape, slash the top with a sharp knife*, brush with some water and let rise another 30-50 minutes. Bake it at 200°C for 20 minutes. Reduce the temperature to 160°C and bake for another 20-30 minutes, until brown and the bread loaf sounds hollow when tapped on the bottom. Makes 1 loaf.

* the dictionary definition of 'bloomer bread' is: a type of large loaf which has diagonal cuts on the top

E. Charlotte potatoes

Ingredients
10 medium sized potatoes
1 cup sour cream
1/2 lb. (225 g) cream cheese
4 tablespoon of butter
1/3 cup chopped chives
paprika, salt & pepper to taste

Instructions
Peel and boil the potatoes until tender. Beat sour cream and cheese together, add hot potatoes and beat until smooth. Add butter, chives, salt, and pepper. Pour into a well greased dish, dot with butter and sprinkle paprika on top. Bake in the oven at 175 degrees for 25 minutes.

F. Caesar salad
Caesar salad is supposed to be named after an Italian, Caesar Cardini, who at the time was a restaurateur in Tijuana, Mexico. According to records, supplies in the restaurant ran short one holiday weekend in 1924. He experimented with the ingredients he had, taking all of them to the table and making the guests feel that they were having the speciality of the house and that evening the Caesar salad was born.
For purists, Caesar salads are made from fresh garlic (used to flavour the oil), cold, dried heart of romaine lettuce leaves, fresh ground pepper, a dash of salt, virgin olive oil, fresh lemon juice, Worcestershire sauce (where the anchovy flavour came from), home-made croutons and Parmesan cheese. The cheese is usually grated in front of the guest at the table.

G. Cajun chicken
See the note in unit 7 task 2.

Activity **9** can usefully be done after the work on the menu.

7 The Sunday lunch wasn't a great success

Aims
– to introduce and give students practice in complaining and apologising
– to give students practice in listening for specific information

a Clarify 'complain' and 'apologise'. For example:
If there is a problem in a restaurant with food, what do you do? – Complain.
If you are the waiter, what should you do? – Apologise, to say sorry.

Play the CD and ask the students to listen for the problems in each of the four dialogues – to fill in the missing words in the problem column at the bottom of page 84.

Tapescripts 7a / Track 35

(key is underlined)

1. *Customer:* Excuse me.
   Barman: Yeah.
   Customer: I ordered a <u>Caesar salad</u> half an hour ago and I'm still waiting for it.
   Barman: <u>Sorry about that.</u> We're short-staffed today. <u>I'll check for you.</u>

2. *Customer:* Excuse me.
   Waiter: Yes. Is everything all right?
   Customer: Well, I ordered the Cajun chicken and it says on the menu it is served with <u>tomato and garlic flat bread</u> but I haven't got any.
   Waiter: <u>I'm sorry about that. I'll get you some now.</u>
   Customer: Thanks.

3. *Customer:* I'm afraid I have a complaint to make.
   Barman: What seems to be the trouble?
   Customer: <u>This fish isn't done in the middle.</u>
   Barman: Oh dear. <u>I really do apologise. Would you like a new portion?</u>
   Customer: No, thanks. I'll have the Cajun chicken instead.
   Barman: Fine. I'm afraid it will take about fifteen minutes.
   Customer: That's OK.

4. *Customer:* Excuse me.
   Barman: Yes?
   Customer: This <u>soup</u> is almost cold.
   Barman: <u>I'm really sorry. I'll send it back.</u> I'll bring you some fresh soup in a minute.

b Check the answers and then play the CD again, this time focussing on the way the waiter apologises. Some problems are more serious than others. Ask students: What is different in the way the waiter apologises for the serious problems and the not so serious ones?

The inclusion of the stressed 'really' in 'I *really* do apologise', 'I'm *really* sorry' and the use of 'apologise' rather than 'I'm sorry ...' makes the apology stronger.
Ask students at random to say the apology sentences to focus on the correct intonation with 'really'. Then ask students to work in pairs and using the **tapescripts** on page 139 act out the dialogues concentrating on the correct intonation for *really*.

c Ask students to decide, working on their own, what apology is appropriate in these situations. Check.

Key 7c

1. I'm sorry about that, I'm really sorry (if it is a *very* expensive coat!)
2. I really do apologise.
3. I really do apologise.
4. Sorry about that. I'm sorry about that.
5. Sorry (I'm late).
6. I really do apologise.

The conversation wouldn't finish there. What did the waiters in **7a** say *after* the apology? Focus on the 'I'll ...'.
Note: this is not a grammatical point for analysis, students learn 'I'll ...' as part of a phrase useful when apologising and offering to put the situation right.
What else would you say in these six situations? Ask students working in pairs to make up the whole conversation for the six situations and then act them out in front of the class if they are willing to do so.

8 The pub lunch

Aim
– to give students practice in responding to polite requests

a Look at the picture. The pub is full so these people are sitting outside. You are going to look at some questions you might ask if you were sitting *inside* a crowded pub where they serve food.

Allow students to look at the questions and possible answers, and then to check with a partner.

Key 8a

?	☺	☹
Can I take this chair?	Sure. Go ahead. / Help yourself.	I'm sorry, it's taken.
Can I look at your menu?	Sure. Here you are. / Help yourself.	Sorry, we need it.
Can I borrow your ashtray?	Sure. Help yourself. / Here you are.	Sorry, we need it.
Can I have the salt and pepper?	Sure. Help yourself. / Here you are.	Sorry, we need it.
Is it OK if I smoke?	Sure. Go ahead.	Well, I'd rather you didn't.
Is it OK if I open a window?	Sure. Go ahead.	Well, I'd rather you didn't.
Can I take your plate?	Sure. Go ahead.	Sorry, I haven't finished yet.

Notice that in asking permission to *do* something 'Sure, go ahead' is used. When you are asking for a concrete *object* that you can be given or can pick up easily you say 'Sure. Here you are.' or 'Help yourself.'

If you want to give students practice using the exponents, ask them to work in pairs. Give each student a dice. One student asks a question and the partner throws the dice. If he/she throws 1, 2 or 3 the response to the partner's request should be a positive one. If the partner throws 4, 5, 6, the response to the request should be a negative one.

UNIT 8

b Stand in a circle with your students who, by this time, are familiar with all the questions and possible answers. Ask, for example: 'Can I take this chair?', throw the ball to a student who has to reply. Then that student has to ask another question and throw the ball to another student and so on. If you feel this activity is superfluous (if you have used the activity with the dice), then it makes a good warmer in the next lesson as it gets tired students up on their feet!

Refer students to exercise **4** in the **back-up section** for more work with apologies.

9 Cherry or sherry?

Aims
- to give students practice in distinguishing between the two sounds [ʃ] and [tʃ]
- to help students make the connection between sound and spelling

a Often students don't make the distinction between two similar sounds because they just don't *hear* the difference. This activity is meant to help them do so.

Play the CD and ask students to repeat the words. You could extend this listening by giving each student a circle of paper and asking them to write [ʃ] on one side and [tʃ] on the other. Then you repeat the words in **9a** *quickly,* jumbled in order and they have to hold up the appropriate side of the paper circle. For example: she's, shoe, chew, cheese, sherry, ships, chips, cherry, chop, shop, sherry, sherry, cherry, chew, shoe, shoe, chew, chips, ships, ships, chips, cheese, she's.
This is a good way of checking whether individuals can hear the difference in sounds, voices *can* get lost if stronger students are shouting out the answers.

Tapescripts 9a / Track 36

1. she's   – cheese
2. sherry   – cherry
3. sheep   – cheap
4. ships   – chips
5. shop   – chop
6. shoe   – chew

b Then play the CD for **9b** so that students have to distinguish which sound they hear. You could also ask them to write down the word they hear as this reinforces the sound spelling association.

Tapescripts 9b / Track 37

1. Cheese, please.
2. Would you like a sherry?
3. This is cheap.
4. The ships are very big.
5. This is an expensive shop.
6. New shoes?

Back-up section

Reference has been made throughout the teacher's notes to the relevant exercises in the back-up section.
The vocabulary activity **3** with missing vowels can form a good warmer for any lesson. Simply choose some words from a previous lesson, remove the vowels and write them on the board or on an OHT. Students have to guess what the words are. When they have done so you can ask them to make sentences with each of the words.

Reference to revision unit

If your students need more practice with modal verbs, look at the reading, writing and language practice sections of the revision unit on pages 104 and 105.

Photocopiable worksheet for unit 8, extra activity (after 4)

She has to take	with crutches.
They have to eat	because you've got a temperature.
She has to walk	because she is pregnant.
He has to go to the dentist's regularly	when she is taking the tablets.
You mustn't eat	a lot of vegetables to stay healthy.
You mustn't go to work today	because I have a fish allergy.
I have to	medicine three times a day.
I mustn't eat salmon	because he has got very bad teeth.
She mustn't drive	take these tablets after meals.
She has to go to the doctor's regularly	sweets if you want to have good teeth.

UNIT 9 Celebrations

Topics:	Special occasions.
Vocabulary:	birthdays, anniversaries, ordinal numbers
Structures:	present perfect and past simple; present progressive for future meaning
Functions:	congratulating
Skills:	reading for detail; listening for detail in a telephone conversation and in an answerphone message
Job Talk:	accepting and refusing invitations
Culture corner:	presents to take to a party; weddings in different countries; optional extra: superstitions concerned with weddings
Reading for fun:	Text 11: Celebrations
Time considerations:	lesson 1: 1 and 2 (with a weak group 1, 2a-c) lesson 2: (2d, e), 3, 4 lesson 3: (3), 5 and 6 Task 3 can be omitted with a weaker group.

Warmer

You could begin by looking at any homework that students have done especially the vocabulary exercise on page 87 or **2b** on page 87.
Alternatively:
Write the word *celebrations* on the board and see how many words students can find in that word.

1 A special date

Aims
– to introduce ordinal numbers
– to give students practice in asking questions in the past tense

a Look at the pictures and decide who is celebrating which birthday. What is special about Lisa's birthday? She was born in a leap year, the year that comes around every four years and has 29 days in February.

Children learn about the months of the year in the little rhyme:
30 days have September,
April, June and November.
All the rest have 31 except February alone
That has 28 days clear
And 29 in each leap year.

b Complete the sentences.

Then write the ordinal numbers from 1st-20th (in figures) on the board and drill them. Point to numbers and ask students at random to repeat them. The problem with these numbers is not so much the words themselves but the pronunciation of them. Firstly, because of the notorious 'th' [θ] and, secondly, because stress placed incorrectly on the words 13 and 30 etc. can lead to serious misunderstandings. It is important, therefore, to have a mechanical phase.

Exercise **2b** on page 94 of the **back-up section** can usefully be done here.

Tapescript 2b back-up / Track 44

1. The next meeting is on the thirteenth of July.
2. It's his fifteenth birthday on Saturday.
3. I'm sorry Mrs Robinson is away until the thirtieth of May.
4. His new daughter was born on the seventeenth of August.
5. His office is on the fourteenth floor.
6. It is their fiftieth wedding anniversary next month.
7. He finished seventieth in the Marathon.
8. Where did you celebrate your fortieth birthday?

c Ask students when they have a birthday and what they did on their last one. Don't go into too much detail here as this will detract from **2a**.

d Give an example of your own so that you can demonstrate rather than explain what to do. Write on the board a date that is important for you, one that you are happy to talk about.
Say: This date is important for me. 13th February 1988. Ask me questions to find out why. I can answer 'yes' or 'no'.

Then ask students to work in groups and to write down three dates that are important for them, exchange them and ask questions to find their significance.

This task gives students the opportunity to practise questions again in the past tense, but it also gives them the opportunity to reveal information about themselves, but the information that they *want* to, not what they are forced to.

2 Birthdays and weddings

Aims
- to introduce and practise the first, second and third person singular forms of the present perfect simple used for the indefinite past
- to show the difference in use between the past simple and the present perfect
- to give students practice in asking questions using both tenses

a The use of present perfect simple has been restricted in this volume to express indefinite time: 'Have you ever ...?' / 'I have never ...' There is an important reason for this. This meaning is the most useful if students are to talk about themselves and their past experience. Other meanings of the tense (the unfinished past used with 'for' and 'since') are either very complicated for students at this level – indeed at any level! – , or are more useful to develop listening skills in the case of a finished event, the results of which are still visible (for example a news broadcast: 'A snow storm has hit Britain.', 'A train has crashed in the west of Ireland.'

Ask students briefly about how they celebrate birthdays or wedding anniversaries? Do they celebrate *every* birthday or only special ones (18, 21, 30, 40, 88?)

Play the CD and draw students' attention to the positive and negative short answers.
Playing the CD allows students to hear the questions repeatedly and the appropriate yes/no answers.

Tapescripts 2a / Track 38

▲ Sandra, have you ever organised a party on a beach?
● Yes, I have.
▲ And have you ever organised a party at the top of a mountain?
● Yes, I have.
▲ And have you ever organised one for more than 100 people?
● For 50 people, yes, but for 100 – no, never.
▲ OK, so one 'no' so far. What about the next question? Have you ever organised a party by a lake?
● Yes, I have.
▲ You obviously like parties. Have you ever organised one by a river?
● Yes, I have.

b Ask: Do we know when she organised all these parties? – No. Some time in the past.
Focus on the form of the verbs. Refer to the **grammar box** on page 90. Then ask students to fill in the information in **2b** on page 89.

c Look at **2c** and show what the task involves. Write on the board: 'Have you ever got drunk in a cathedral?'

Ask: This is a possible sentence. The grammar is right, but is it sensible? (Be careful: you may need to point out that sensible means 'vernünftig' in German and not 'sensibel!')

In fact if the students can justify *why* some other wacky suggestions are possible then so much the better! They are thinking *and* having fun.

Allow students to make up their sentences. Move around and ask them to refer back to the questions in **2a** and draw attention to how the questions were answered with 'Yes, I have' or 'No, never'. Then ask students to move around the class and ask the questions.

The feedback session allows students, in a natural way, to focus on the full forms of the positive and negative sentences.

Key 2c

Have you ever celebrated a birthday/a wedding anniversary
– on a beach?
– at the top of a mountain?
– in a beer garden?
– on a ship?
– in Hawaii?
– by a lake/by a river?

Have you ever attended a wedding
– in a cathedral?
– on a ship?
– in Hawaii?
– of friends from a different culture?

Have you ever given a speech
– at party/ at a wedding?

Have you ever got drunk
– in a beer garden?
– at a party/at a wedding?

d The contrast between the present perfect simple and the simple past has been restricted to the verb 'to be'. This is for two reasons. Firstly, the manipulation of forms between the past simple and the present perfect simple is a difficult one to master at first, particularly at this level. Students need to be able to concentrate on the new material – the form of the present perfect simple. Secondly, it is, in fact, more natural to ask follow-up questions with the verb 'to be' than with another main verb.
For example:
Have you ever eaten caviar?
Yes, I have.
When/where was that? (rather than: When did you eat caviar)
In Moscow in 2003. (rather than: I ate caviar in Moscow in 2003)

Work done here can be built on in *English Elements 3* and *English Elements 4*. If students don't go on learning English having finished this volume, they will still be able to talk about their past experience and be an interested listener.

Play the dialogue and allow the students to fill in the missing words.

Tapescripts 2d / Track 39

▲ Have you ever given a speech at a wedding?
● Yes, I have.
▲ When was that?
● At my brother's wedding in 2002.

In normal conversations we don't just ask one question after the other and answer 'yes' or 'no'. If we find something interesting, we ask more questions. We want some definite information to answer our questions: 'what', 'when', 'why', 'where' and 'when' we want this information, we use the past tense.

e Put students in groups. The **photocopiable activity on page 96** can help you to do this.

Procedure
1. This activity works best with groups of four or three, but you *could* have students working in pairs, although then the idea of the 'hot seat' is lost. If you have anxious students, you can leave out this element of stress anyway!
2. Copy the worksheet and cut up the sentences into the indicated parts. Some sentences have only two parts, some have three and some have four.

3. In class give each student a cut-up part of a sentence and ask them to find their partner(s) by finding people who have words that could make a sentence with their word or words. Question marks are important!
4. Sit down in this new group or pair.

Ask the students to follow the instructions on page 90 in the student's book.

3 Wedding customs

Aims
- to give students practice in reading for detail
- to continue the topic of celebrations
- to encourage students to share their knowledge of the world (in this case about weddings)

For details as to how to handle this sort of reading activity see the description for task **7** in unit 2 on page 21 in this book.

This task can be left out if time is short and your class is not very interested in the subject matter.

You may need to pre-teach some vocabulary.

<u>Indian wedding</u>

vow	a serious promise
showers	(here) throws
petals	parts of a flower (draw them!)
protect	keep them safe
evil	the opposite of good
jewellery	rings, earrings, necklaces (this last word is also new; try drawings to make meaning clear)
stain	if you spill coffee on your skirt it will stain it
henna	a brown colouring (students may know it from hair colour products)
groom	a man on his wedding day
gift	present

<u>Mexican wedding</u>

godparents	people who promise to help you on the day of your christening (Taufe) and through your whole life
ribbon	young girls often tie up their hair with this
rosary	Catholics use this when they pray (talk to God)
a coin	metal money (paper money is a note)
beads	small round pieces of glass or stone
paper mache	paper cut up into small pieces and mixed with glue to make models
ceiling	the top of a room
share	everyone has part of them (the sweets are for *all* guests, not just for one person)

Extra activity
This activity prepares students to meet the first conditional in unit 10 and it is concerned with superstitions including ones about weddings.

Procedure
1. Make enough copies of the **photocopiable worksheet on page 97** so that each student has one.
2. Put students into pairs.
3. Explain the idea of 'superstitions'. You can use the following example if you wish:
   If the groom sees his bride in her wedding dress before their wedding, this will bring bad luck.
4. Give students the worksheet. Explain the words: 'itch', 'spill', 'robin' and ask them, in pairs, to order the parts of the sentences from column A and B to make superstitions.
5. Have a feedback session and discuss other superstitions that the students know if you have a class that is receptive to the idea.

Key

If you marry in blue,
→ you will always be true
If you marry on a Tuesday,
→ you will have a lot of money.
If a woman sees a robin on Valentine's Day,
→ she will marry a sailor.
If you break a mirror,
→ you will have seven years' bad luck.
If your nose itches,
→ you will have a visitor.
If you spill some pepper,
→ you will have an argument with a friend.
If you put salt on the door of a new house,
→ it will keep the devil away.
If you say goodbye to a friend on a bridge,
→ you will never see each other again.

9

4 Away on honeymoon

Aim
– to introduce and practise the present continuous used to express definite future arrangements

Background information
The name 'honeymoon' dates back to times when a man 'stole' his wife from her parents' home and took her away before the wedding. The couple also hid from the bride's parents for a cycle of the moon (a month) *after* the wedding during which time they drank honey wine.

Extra activity
Copy the diary on the **photocopiable worksheet on page 98** onto an overhead transparency. Display it and elicit the words 'diary' and 'appointment'. Show your diary and say 'This is a …? – A diary.' and 'What do you write in your diary? – Appointments, things you don't want to forget, etc.'
If students say 'date' when they mean 'appointment', the following might make it clear:
d ♥ te.

Then focus on some of the appointments and say what the person is doing at various times.
Do you think it is a woman's diary or a man's?! It is assumed here that it is a woman's diary.

Key to extra activity

She's collecting Robert from the airport on Monday.
She's going to a parent's meeting on Monday evening.
She's having lunch with Peter at 1.30 on Tuesday.
She's flying to Munich on Tuesday evening.
She's having a meeting (going to a meeting) at a brewery all day on Wednesday.
She's flying back to London on Wednesday evening.
She's going to her Italian lesson at half past seven on Thursday evening.
She's going to the dentist's on Friday morning.
She's going to the cinema (with her children). / She's taking the children to the cinema on Saturday afternoon.
She's going to Roger's christening on Sunday. (christening – this word comes in exercise 3 in the back-up section, so point it out here.)

a By displaying the diary you can point out the connection between the entry in the diary and the use of the present continuous in the dialogue. It reinforces the fact that the students don't need to write full sentences when they listen to the dialogue on the CD.

Play the CD and ask the students to fill in the fixed points in the week.

Tapescripts 4a / Track 40

Dorothy: Norwich 48026
Joan: Hello, Dot. This is Joan.
Dorothy: Oh, hello Joan. How are you?
Joan: Fine, thanks. And you? Is your cold better?
Dorothy: Yes, I'm fine now, thanks. Are you coming next Tuesday?
Joan: 'Fraid not. That's why I'm ringing. You know Sarah's getting married again on Saturday?
Dorothy: Yes. Is everything alright?
Joan: Yes, everything's fine with Sarah and Alec, but it's Tim. He's going into hospital and he can't look after the children, so we're collecting them on the Monday and then on Tuesday we're taking them to The Anfield experience.
Dorothy: Oh, you mean the tour round the Liverpool football ground. So no golf on Tuesday this week then. And Wednesday?
Joan: Well, we're not doing anything special, but we won't have time to see you I'm afraid.
Dorothy: So when are Sarah and Alec coming back?
Joan: On Monday the 22nd at 7 in the evening. So no golf on Saturday 20th either, I'm afraid.
Dorothy: Ah, well. Never mind. By the way have you ever taken the kids to the Blue Planet Aquarium or to the Llangollen horse-drawn canal boat centre? I've never been, but my grandson Sam has. It was with his school last summer and he had a wonderful time.
Joan: Oh, I'm glad because I've never been, but we're going to Llangollen on Saturday and to the aquarium on Monday.
Dorothy: I'm sure the kids will enjoy it.
Joan: I hope so. So I'll see you on the 13th for the big day.

Dorothy: Yes. Fingers crossed that it doesn't rain and that 13 is a lucky number! Bye.
Joan: Bye.

Check the answers and at this point students should use whole sentences using the -ing form.

Key 4a

diary entry	whole sentences using -ing form
– Sarah's wedding	Sarah is getting married on Saturday.
– collect the children	Joan's collecting the children on Monday.
– Liverpool football club	They are going to the Liverpool football club on Tuesday.
– Cheshire ice cream farm	On Thursday they're going to the Cheshire ice cream farm.
– Llangollen	On Saturday Joan is taking the children to Llangollen.
– Blue Planet Aquarium / Sarah and Alec come back	On Monday they are going to the Blue Planet Aquarium and Sarah and Alec are coming back from their honeymoon.
– take the kids back to Stockport	On Tuesday Joan is taking the children back home.

b, c Now ask students to draw a 'diary' on a piece of paper and to write in it what they are doing in the next few days. They don't have to be absolutely truthful! Then students work in pairs and ask each other 'What are you doing on …?'

5 The invitation

Aims
– to give students practice in listening for specific information and note-taking
– to give students practice in leaving messages
– to give more practice in the use of the present continuous.
– to give practice in the use of language exponents used on the telephone

a Ask how many students have an answering machine on their phone or in their mobile mail box. Do they listen to their messages as soon as they get home?

Play the CD and ask students to make a note of the message.

Tapescripts 5a / Track 41

(key underlined)

Hello. You have reached Henley 9846721. Peter and Alison Gladstone can't take your call at the moment, but if you leave your name and number we'll ring you back as soon as possible.

Hello. This is Janie Clayton speaking. I'm <u>Mr Bradbury's assistant</u>. As you know <u>Mr Bradbury is retiring</u> at the end of next month after 40 years with the company. I hope you have received <u>the invitation to the cocktail party on Friday 15th July at 6 p.m</u>. Could you ring me back as soon as possible to let me know if <u>you can attend</u>? My number is <u>020 457 9821</u>. Thank you.

Key 5a

Notepad
Message from: Mr Bradbury's assistant
Message: Mr Bradbury retiring
Cocktail party 15th July 6.p.m.
Can you attend?
Phone: 0204579821

So can you go to the cocktail party? Clarify the meaning of 'accept = yes' and 'refuse = no'. Students may need help with the pronunciation of 'unfortunately'.
Ask for some suggestions as to reasons for refusing an invitation. This reinforces the present progressive for arrangements and gives students some ideas for when they come to write their own messages.

b Then ask students to do two things.

1. Write their message, following the suggestions in **5b**.
2. Make up Mr Bradbury's assistant's answering machine message.

Ask students to work in pairs sitting back to back. One student gives the answering machine introduction and the other one then leaves their message. Then students change roles.
If you have a small class and access to a cassette recorder, it is fun to actually record the messages and then listen to them. With a big class this may take up too much time and be impractical.

Key 5b

(suggested messages)

Accept

Hello, this is Mr/Mrs Gladstone. That's G-L-A-D-S-T-O-N-E.
I'm very sorry we haven't replied to the invitation. We were on holiday and came back yesterday. We would be delighted to accept the kind invitation. We look forward to attending the party on Friday 15th.

Refuse

Hello …
Unfortunately, we can't attend the party as we are going to my father's 80th birthday party on that day. Please send our good wishes to Mr Bradbury.

c Refer back to the information in unit 3 on how to answer the phone in different countries.
Then look at the tapescript on page 139 and notice how Dorothy answers the phone, with the number. Then what do the friends do?
This 'small talk' before the main business of the phone call is important (e.g. How are you? – Fine, thanks, and you? –Fine, too.)

Students are going to work in pairs and make a phone call. One person is going to phone to accept or refuse the invitation and the other partner is going to react to the call. How *will* they react to good news (accept the invitation) or to bad news (refuse the invitation)?

☺
Great. See you on Saturday.
Good, looking forward to seeing you.

☹
Sorry you can't come. See you soon I hope.
That's a shame. (point out that the meaning of 'shame' in German is 'schade' and not 'Schande').
Oh, well. Never mind.

Students work in pairs and make the call.

6 At the party

Aims
– to give practice in responding to small talk heard at a party
– to talk about what behaviour is accepted at parties in different cultures

a, b Ask students to match sentences from column A with ones from column B and then to listen to the CD to check.

Tapescripts 6b / Track 42

▲ Hi. Sorry, I'm late. The traffic was very bad.
● No problem. Go through and help yourself to a drink.
▲ Thanks.

▲ Can I take your coat?
● Oh, yes. Thank you.

▲ Would you like another drink?
● Yes, please, but just something soft. I'm driving.
▲ Orange juice OK?
● Fine.

▲ What a pretty blouse. The colour suits you.
● Thank you. Nice of you to say so.

▲ Congratulations.
● Thanks.

▲ Thanks for a lovely evening.
● Not at all. Thank you for coming. Drive carefully.
▲ I will. Bye.
● Bye.

▲ The food is wonderful.
● Thanks. I'm glad you like it.

Note that there are some extra words in the little dialogues that are not on the page.
Then students can work in pairs and practise the dialogues.

Also discuss the questions in the **culture corner** section at the bottom of page 93.

Background information
In Saudi Arabia don't admire something too much as the host might feel obliged to give it to you. You only give presents to very good friends. To receive presents from a lesser acquaintance is embarrassing and can even be offensive. The receiver will open the present immediately and examine it minutely.

In Arabian countries gifts made of wood are of very low status – they will dry out fast and won't last very long.

Similarly in Mexico where silver is abundant, gifts of silver are of very low status.

In Japan gifts should be given with both hands and the person giving the gift says how small or unimportant the gift is: tsumaranai mon (an uninteresting or dull thing). This conveys the feeling that 'our relationship is more important than this small gift'. Gifts are opened in private. Avoid pairs of anything as this is unlucky and don't send red greetings cards as funeral notices are sent in red.

In Russia you should give an odd number of flowers as even numbers are associated with funerals. Pink, cream, orange or blue are neutral colours and so safe choices!

In Britain wine, champagne, flowers or chocolates are appropriate gifts, but not spirits. Avoid giving red roses (for lovers), white lilies or chrysanthemums (used in funerals).

Find out more on the web-site:
www.1worldglobalgifts.com

Reference to revision unit

If your students need more practice with the present perfect, look at the speaking section in the revision unit on page 105.

Photocopiable worksheet for unit 9, after 2e

For groups of three

We have never	climbed	a high mountain.
They have never	eaten	snails.
Have you ever	driven	a tractor?

For groups of four

She has never	had	a car	accident.
I have never	drunk	champagne	for breakfast.
Have you ever	met	a famous	person?

For pairs

I have never	eaten caviar.
Have you ever	broken your leg?

Photocopiable worksheet for unit 9, extra activity (after 3)

Column A	Column B
If you marry in blue,	you will never see each other again.
If you marry on a Tuesday,	you will have an argument with a friend.
If a woman sees a robin on Valentine's Day,	it will keep the devil away.
If you break a mirror,	you will have a lot of money.
If your nose itches,	you will always be true.
If you spill some pepper,	she will marry a sailor.
If you put salt on the door of a new house,	you will have seven years' bad luck.
If you say goodbye to a friend on a bridge,	you will have a visitor.

Photocopiable worksheet for unit 9, extra activity (for 4)

Monday	collect Robert from the airport 10.15	parents' meeting at school 7 p.m.
Tuesday	lunch with Peter 1.30	Munich EasyJet flight EZY 3415 18.20
Wednesday	meeting at brewery 8 a.m – 5 p.m.	London Stansted EasyJet flight EZY 3416 21.15
Thursday		Italian lesson 7.30
Friday	dentist 10.45 a.m.	
Saturday		Harry Potter and the Prisoner of Azkaban 3.p.m
Sunday	Roger's christening 11a.m.	

UNIT 10 What does the future hold?

Topics:	Talking about the future with particular reference to future developments in homes and housing.
Vocabulary:	homes, furniture, technology
Structures:	prepositions of place; will-future to express predictions; going to-future to express plans; if sentences type 1
Functions:	making predictions; saying goodbye
Skills:	reading for detail; listening for gist in a song
Culture corner:	homes in other countries
Learning tip:	how to go on learning English after the course; collecting 'spoken' language
Reading for fun:	Text 12: Have a holiday in a historic building
Time considerations:	lesson 1: 1-4 (a good group may discuss longer in task 1; a weaker group might need more time for the reading)
	lesson 2: 5, 6
	lesson 3: 7 and 8 plus vocabulary revision from the back-up section

If you are under time pressure, you can omit 1 and 5 and so reduce the time taken to two double lessons.

1 What couldn't you live without in your home?

Aims
– to introduce the topic of homes and technology
– to encourage the students to talk
– to give students at this level a framework in which they can talk

a Houses change. Our great-grandmothers (clarify the word) didn't have dishwashers. Ask how many people in the class have a dishwasher now. Could they live without it? Of course they could, but would they *want* to?!
Ask students to look at the list of things you can find in a modern home. Which couldn't they live without. Encourage them to add ideas of their own.

b Then students work in pairs and tell each other *why* these things are important to them.
Give an example to show what is required:
'I couldn't live without an alarm clock because I am not a morning sort of person and would often oversleep if I didn't have an alarm clock. I don't like mornings and I have to get up early.'

As the pairs are discussing, monitor and ask them later to share any ideas you heard that were interesting.

2 Furniture

Aims
– to introduce vocabulary in the lexical set of furniture
– to introduce the prepositions of place

Brainstorm as many words for furniture as possible. The word 'furniture' can pose problems for learners of English because it is an uncountable noun and cannot be used in the plural. You may hear students saying 'furnitures'. The way you present the new words might help to solve this problem.

10

chair		table
bed		lamp
fire place	FURNITURE	picture
coffee table		bookshelves
writing desk		wardrobe
sofa		

Make sure you include the words needed for task **2a**.

Before students can do task **2a** they need to understand prepositions of place: above, against, behind, between, in front of, next to, on, opposite, to the left of, to the right of, under.

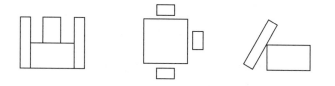

If you have a set of Cuisenaire rods – small blocks of different coloured wood – , you can position them so that you can make the meaning of the prepositions clear. You can also explain the shapes 'square' and 'rectangular' with these rods. These two words come in the reading text later.

Then ask students to do task **2a**.

Key

1. true
2. false (the lamp is next to the chair)
3. true
4. false (to the right of the TV against the wall on the floor next to the fireplace)
5. false (in front of the sofa)
6. true
7. true
8. false (under the TV on the carpet)

Check and answer the questions.

3 The house of the future

Aims
– to continue on the topic of furniture and houses
– to give students practice in reading for detail
– to introduce passively the will-future for predictions

a-c This is the most difficult of the reading texts in the book, logical as this is the last unit.

If you have a weak group, you might like to have an extra phase in the reading lesson. Ask them to look through the text very quickly and to pick out all the furniture words that they can find, and words for parts of the house.

You should at any event pre-teach the following:

have changed	are different now
influence	to make something change
to afford	to have enough money
dims the lights	to make the room darker
chooses	to decide which one you want
to suit your mood	If you are happy, maybe yellow and red suit your mood, or you are sad, maybe blue and green suits your mood. (You can ask the students what colour they like when they are sad or happy.)
suitable	a one-room flat is not suitable for a family of five
solve	If you solve a problem, you don't have a problem anymore.
on the contrary	quite the opposite
spoil	make it less attractive
protect	to keep danger from someone
unusual	strange, not that you see every day
square	draw the shape!
rectangular	draw the shape!
invent	Edison invented the light bulb; Diesel invented the engine
penknife	a Swiss army knife is a sort of penknife
floor-length	so long that they touch the floor
storage space	place where you put your clothes, your papers

Students should then read the text so that they can see which predictions from **3a** were borne out in the reading text.
Have a feedback session and then ask the students to read the text again more carefully and to answer the questions in **3c**. Check the answers.

Key 3c

1. There will be a lot more technology because it will be cheaper and more efficient.
2. It is very expensive.
3. They won't come to your home to make repairs, they will do it by computer.
4. Because humans need stimulation.
5. Business professionals will travel more often and they won't stay in hotels, they will take their home with them.

d Then have a discussion phase. Answer the questions in **3d**.

Background information
Homes in other countries
You could simply ask the class to give you as many words for home as they know and expand on this or you could ask for students' experiences of different homes that they have visited when they were on holiday.
For example:
A great example of houses underground is in the opal mining town of Coober Pedy in Australia. It is so hot that a lot of houses and even a hotel are built underground. For pictures go to:
www.opalcapitaloftheworld.com.au

Wigwams and tepees are homes of native Americans both designed so that they could be moved easily. A wigwam was a covered wooden frame shaped like a cone.
The tepee was made of long wooden poles pointed together and fastened at the top, the bottoms were spread out to form a circle. This was covered with a tent of animal skins which fastened to the ground.

Some of your students may have been on holiday and seen other types of tents, the Yurts of Mongolia for example, or visited exhibitions with examples of them.

Many other students may have been on holidays to Asia where it is customary to take off your shoes before entering a private home and where, in country villages particularly, many houses are built on stilts for animals to live under the house and to avoid the danger of snakes.

The discussion can be as superficial or as detailed as your students wish it to be.

If you have classes that are really interested in the subject, it is worth investing a book:
'Houses and Homes around the World' (in the Around the World Series) by Ann Morris and Ken Heyman, published by Harper Trophy. It has beautiful illustrations.

4 Over to you

Aim
– to allow students to use the grammar to make their own predictions

The grammar here is treated very much as lexical grammar and not as a grammar point to be dissected and analysed.
There are no right answers to these questions and the model has been given so that it is very likely that students will get the grammar right.

There are the following suggestions in the key. It must be stressed, however, that these are only suggestions.

Key 4

We think that the price of petrol will rise to over 2 Euro a litre / stabilise at 1.25 / 1.50 / will be more expensive/cheaper in the future
We think the price of flats in our cities will rise.
We think the average temperature next summer will be 30°.
We think air in cities will get cleaner / dirtier in the future.
We think the number of cars on our roads will increase / fall.
We think that we will eat more vegetables / fast food / genetically modified food in the future.

With a good group you could ask them for their own predictions about the future, about any subject that interests them.

10

5 I want to move

Aim
- to introduce and give practice in the first conditional used to express possible conditions

If you wish students to move to talk to someone new and not the person they always sit next to, the line-up is an appropriate way of getting them into new pairs. Ask students to line up according to the name of the street where they live.
They have to ask 'What's your address?' and line up with an address with A at one side of the room and one with Z at the other.
So someone who lives in 'Adenauer-Allee' will stand at one end of the line and one who lives in 'Zeppelin-Straße' will stand at the other. Then ask the students to sit with the person next to them.

Talk about living in this street and what they like and dislike about it. For example: It is noisy because there is a lot of traffic but it is very convenient. It is near a good supermarket and the underground station.

Then set the scene that someone wants to move from the city to the country. Look at the examples and the **grammar box** on page 99.

With a good class at this stage of the course you shouldn't need to help anymore than this. If you have a weaker group, however, you could brainstorm advantages and disadvantages before you set the students the task of talking about advantages and disadvantages.

Key 5

(some possible answers)
If you move to the country, you'll
- spend more money on travelling to work / on petrol.
- need a car.
- have a garden.
- have a bigger flat.
- be healthier.

If you move to the town, you'll (you won't)
- spend more money on entertainment.
- go to the theatre more often.
- need a car.
- use public transport more often.
- spend more money on food.

Refer students to exercise **1** on page 102 in the **back-up section** which has more work on if-clauses. The listening section in the **revision unit** on page 105 also deals with the first conditional.

6 A house or a home?

Aims
- to have fun listening to a song
- to raise awareness of how different spellings can have the same sound

a Discuss the questions in **6a**.

b Ask students to work individually and to match the words that have the same sounds. Then ask them to compare answers with a partner. Then play the CD to check the answers so that the students hear the words before they hear them in the song. Clarify any vocabulary necessary.

buffoon = a fool
frown = the opposite of 'to smile'
curls = you can have straight hair or hair with curls, curly hair
a frock = a dress

There is some colloquial language in this song, particularly in the first verse.

to be on the make = to try very hard to get more power and money
to be on the bum = a bum is a person who doesn't have a job or a proper home and lives by asking other people for money
I've looned = played the fool

Tapescripts 6b / Track 45

breaks	–	mistakes
around	–	town
free	–	me
moon	–	buffoon
frowns	–	clowns
land	–	hand
girls	–	curls

c Play the CD and ask students to put the lines in order as they hear the song. Alternatively, you can copy the text from the **photocopiable worksheet on page 105** and ask the students working in pairs to reconstruct what they think is the order, bearing in mind that there are rhymes in the text.

Then you can play the CD to check and a second time so that the students can listen for the answers to the questions: Why is the man running for home? There is, of course, no one correct answer (e.g. Has he lost all his money? Has he broken up with a partner? Has he lost his job? Has he been round the world and now he is coming home?)

d Students might associate a certain piece of music with an event or time in their life. This is a case when they should not be *forced* to share. It helps if you can share a piece of music that is special to *you*.

Extra activity
In England there is a programme called 'Desert Island Discs' in which a famous personality is asked to talk about his or her life and to choose the ten pieces of music they would like to have if they were shipwrecked on a desert island. You could ask your students to choose two such pieces of music each and explain why. They could also play the music!

Some ideas might be:
– This piece of music reminds me of my father, because it was his favourite piece of music.
– This is my favourite piece of music because the organ played it at our wedding.
– I like this piece of music because I bought a CD of it when I got my first pay cheque!
– This music reminds me of a wonderful holiday in Spain.

7 So now what?

Aims
– to introduce (for passive understanding) the going to-future used to express plans
– to encourage learners to consider how they are going to continue learning outside the classroom

Snoopy is going to do something new, so what are they going to do? What are their plans for the future?

Ask students to look at the suggestions and to choose which one(s) appeal to them.

If you have enthusiastic 'surfers' in your class, you can suggest the following web-sites (current January 2005).

www.better-english.com/exericselist.html
www.aitech.ac.jp/~iteslj/quizzes/vocabulary.html
www.allwords.com
www.word-detective.com
The on-line version of a magazine 'The Word Detective'. Probably more use to you as a teacher as it is very wordy, if you will excuse the pun.

If you have the time, exercise **4** on page 103 in the **back-up section** can usefully be done in class time as this encourages students to look back through the whole book and so it reinforces the fact that the book is a useful resource that they can take away with them at the end of the course. Having to decide which words they like and don't like brings the emotional intelligence of the learners into play. There are, of course, no right or wrong answers and so this will not appeal to all learners!

Refer students to exercise **2** on page 102 in the **back-up section** that deals with ways of expressing the future.

8 It's time to say goodbye

Aims
– to round off the course in an appropriate way
– to present students with some useful phrases for saying goodbye
– to expose students to some informal ways of saying goodbye that they might hear in the UK

Ask students to match ways of saying goodbye with appropriate responses.
Then play the CD to check. You can ask them if they can think of a situation in which these little exchanges would be appropriate.

Tapescripts 8 / Track 47

1. ▲ Goodbye. Thank you for inviting me.
   ● Thank you for coming. Drive carefully. Goodbye.

   (Saying goodbye at the end of a party.)

2. ▲ Bye, Bill. Give our love to Angela.
   ● I will. Bye.

   (Anytime – friends saying goodbye.)

3. ▲ I hope you soon settle into your new home. Keep in touch.
   ● Thanks. We will.

   (Neighbours saying goodbye when someone is moving flat/house.)

4. ▲ Bye. Have a good flight.
   ● Thanks.
   ▲ Give us a ring when you arrive in Sydney.
   ● Yes, I will. Bye.

   (Friends/relatives saying goodbye to someone at the airport.)

5. ▲ Good night. Sleep well.
   ● Thanks, you too.

   (An exchange before you go to bed.)

6. ▲ Cheers mate. I'm off home now.
   ● Yeah. Cheers. See you tomorrow.

(A colleague going home. Very informal language – probably said by a younger person probably male and under 30 rather than someone over 40! 'Cheers' can now mean 'goodbye' as well as the traditional thing you say before you drink a beer with friends.)

Key 8

1.c, 2.d, 3.f, 4.a, 5.b, 6.e

There are more dialogues about saying goodbye in the **back-up section** on page 103.

Choose a way of saying goodbye that you think is appropriate and say goodbye to your students!

Photocopiable worksheet for unit 10, 6c

I've travelled the land
With a guitar in my hand
And an eye ever open for some fun.
I've made some mistakes
Had my share of the breaks
Seen the boys on the make
And on the bum.
Run for home
Run as fast as I can
Oh, running man
Running for home
I've seen all the frowns
On the faces of the clowns
And the downs that they take
Just to be free.
I've seen all the girls
In their pretty frocks and curls
But they don't mean a lot to me.
Run for home ...
I've been to the places in the town
Where the faces hang around
Just to stare at each other.
I've looned with them
Screamed at the moon
Behaved like a buffoon
But I soon discovered.
Run for home ...
I've travelled the land
Made mistakes out of hand
Seen the faces in the places misunderstand.
I've been round the world
Seen the pretty boys and girls
Heard the noise
That destroys and commands.

Reading for fun

The following is a collection of reading texts that tell something about Britain. Students don't have to answer questions on these reading texts. They should go home and read them just for fun. Difficult words are underlined and translated at the bottom of each reading text. You can handle these texts in various different ways.

1. You can photocopy them – (two copies of each for a big class), laminate them and put them in a class library so that students can help themselves when they feel like it.
2. You can copy the appropriate text when the unit that it roughly refers to has been covered and hand it out to your students.
3. You can, of course, do work with them in class time, but beware of merely reading them and then translating them as this would defeat the object of the exercise. The texts are supposed to encourage reading for fun!

Reading for fun

1 Surnames

You have got it in your passport, on your credit card, in your driving licence. We have all got two or maybe more than two. – Names.
Why have most people got at least one first name and a surname? – Because in the 12th century there were three very common names for men: William, Richard and John. So there were problems for visitors in towns and villages! "Hello, is William here?" – "William number one, two, three or four?" The answer to the problem was surnames.

"Hello, is William here?" – "John's son?"
"Is William here?" – "The miller?"
"Is William here?" – "The one who lives near the hill."
"Hello, is William here?" – "The one who's got very long legs."

So suddenly it was no problem to know which person the visitor wanted to talk to: William Johnson, William Miller, William Hill and William Long. Later, all these Williams gave these new names to their children and their children's children and this was the beginning of surnames.

Surnames can tell you a lot of information about your ancestors. 'Mac' in Scotland means 'son of'.
So one of Duncan Mac Donald's ancestors was 'Donald's son'.
'O' in Ireland means 'grandson of'. So one of Rory O'Grady's ancestors was 'Grady's grandson'.
Surnames can tell you something about the job one of your ancestors had. One of Mrs Thatcher's ancestors made straw roofs or thatched roofs for houses, they were thatchers.
Surnames can also tell you about the area where your ancestors lived. Tony Blair's ancestors lived near a field because the old word 'blar' meant 'field'. Your surname can also tell you about the nickname of your ancestors. John White's ancestors had white hair, maybe.

If you want to find out more about names, you can look on the web-site
http://surnames.behindthename.com

ancestors	*Vorfahren*	*means, meant*	*bedeutet, bedeutete*
century	*Jahrhundert*	*miller*	*Müller*
common	*geläufig*	*nickname*	*Kosename, Rufname*
driving licence	*Führerschein*	*straw roofs*	*Strohdächer*
field	*Feld*	*suddenly*	*auf einmal*
gave	*gaben*	*thatchers*	*(Stroh-) Dachdecker*
hair	*Haare*	*villages*	*Dörfer*
hill	*Hügel*	*visitors*	*Besucher*
legs	*Beine*	*wanted*	*wollte*
maybe	*vielleicht*		

Reading for fun

2 Soccer or football?

People play football in many <u>different</u> countries and there are a lot of different rules for the game. There are rules for Rugby football, for American football, for Australian football and for Association football, the football that is also <u>called</u> soccer.

Why do some people say they play soccer and not football? In the 1880s students at Oxford <u>used</u> a <u>special</u> short form for some words and this short form ended in -er. So they said 'brekker' and not 'breakfast', 'rugger' and not 'rugby'.
A friend <u>asked</u> one student, Charles Wreford, "Do you want to play rugger?" and he answered, "No, soccer." This was the short form for Association football.

<u>Between</u> 1307 and 1327 if the <u>authorities</u> <u>caught</u> someone playing football, they <u>went to prison</u>. When King Henry IV and Henry VIII were kings football was forbidden. When Queen Elizabeth I was queen football players went to prison for a week and then they <u>had to</u> go to church on Sunday to say they were <u>sorry</u> for this <u>bad behaviour</u>.

But <u>laws</u> didn't stop people who wanted to play football and in 1681 it <u>became</u> legal to play football in England. The <u>earliest</u> rules of the game were from Eton College in 1815. Now <u>teams</u> play soccer all over the <u>world</u> and it is a very <u>popular</u> sport, <u>more</u> people watch the Soccer World Cup than the Olympic Games.

authorities	Obrigkeit, (Staats)gewalt	laws	Gesetze
asked	fragte	more	mehr
bad behaviour	schlechtes Benehmen	popular	beliebt
became	wurde	rules	Regeln
between	zwischen	say sorry	sich entschuldigen
called	genannt	special	besonderen
caught	ertappten	teams	Mannschaften
different	verschiedene	used	benutzten
earliest	frühesten	world	Welt
had to	mussten	went to prison	ins Gefängnis gehen

Reading for fun

3 The milkman

Milk and beer are very special drinks in Britain. Why? – Because you can buy a pint of beer and a pint of milk (a pint is 0.473176 litre), but you can't buy a pint of <u>engine oil</u> or orange juice, you buy litres.

You can, of course, buy milk in a supermarket in a <u>carton</u> or <u>plastic bottle</u>, but you can also buy it from your <u>local</u> milkman (milk lady or milk delivery person) in a glass bottle. He or she gets up <u>early</u> and drives in a van from house to house and <u>delivers</u> milk to <u>customers</u> every morning. And not only milk. You can also buy orange juice, <u>cream</u>, butter and eggs and sometimes cheese and bread from the milkman. At Christmas some milkmen <u>sell</u> <u>turkeys</u> for Christmas dinner. Customers <u>pay</u> the milkman once a week.

The milkman is <u>like</u> the red <u>telephone box</u>. This job is <u>typically</u> British. But life <u>is changing</u> and there are problems for the traditional British milkman. Old people who haven't got a car and who live in villages where there isn't a supermarket often <u>rely on</u> the milkman to bring them milk and food, but a lot of people buy their milk from the supermarket because it is <u>cheaper</u> or because all the people in the family <u>go out to work</u> <u>all day</u> or go to school from 9 o'clock in the morning until four o'clock in the afternoon and it is not good to <u>leave</u> the milk on the <u>doorstep</u> in the sun in the summer. So, <u>unfortunately</u>, there isn't a milkman in every town and village in Britain now.

all day	den ganzen Tag	*like*	(hier): wie
carton	Karton	*once*	einmal
changing	ändert sich	*pay*	bezahlen
cheaper	billiger	*rely on*	sich auf etwas verlassen
cream	Sahne	*sell*	verkaufen
customers	Kunden	*telephone box*	Telefonzelle
deliver	liefern	*turkey*	Truthahn
doorstep	Türschwelle	*typically*	typisch
early	früh	*unfortunately*	leider
go out to work	außer Haus arbeiten	*until*	bis
leave	(hier): stehen lassen	*van*	Lieferwagen

Reading for fun

4 The city of Bath in England

A lot of people today go on 'wellness' holidays. They have massages and they relax in hot baths and eat healthy food and sometimes they drink special water that is good for them.

People do this in the city of Bath in the south-west of England. Bath is a World Heritage Site, like the Pyramids and it is famous for its Roman Baths and for its hot springs, the only ones in Britain. From 600 BC to 400 AD it was a Roman town called 'Aquae Sulis'.

Many famous people visited Bath to drink the spa waters. The most famous was Queen Victoria. She drank three glasses of the water every morning before breakfast.

But Bath is also famous for another reason. The first letter with a stamp on it was posted in Bath in 1840.

Today, many tourists visit this city to see the Roman Baths, the Pump Room where you can drink the water, and the many beautiful buildings.

buildings	Gebäude	400 AD	400 nach Christus
drank	trank	was posted	wurde aufgegeben
good for them	tut Ihnen gut		(eingeworfen), gesendet
famous	berühmt	reason	Grund
hot springs	heiße Quellen	stamp	Briefmarke
like	(hier) sowie	visited	besuchte
the only ones	die einzigen	World Heritage Site	Weltkulturdenkmal
600 BC	600 vor Christus		

Reading for fun

5 Shrove Tuesday (Pancake Day)

Shrove Tuesday is the Tuesday before Ash Wednesday, the first day of <u>Lent</u>, the forty days before Easter. The name comes from an old English irregular verb 'shrive' (shrove, shriven) which means 'to say sorry' and '<u>be forgiven</u>'.

Shrove Tuesday is a time of <u>celebrations</u> before Lent and is often called 'Pancake Day'. In the <u>past</u> there was a lot of <u>food</u> that Christians didn't eat in Lent – meat, fish, <u>fats</u>, eggs and milky food. So on Shrove Tuesday families had a <u>feast</u> of <u>pancakes</u> before they had to say 'goodbye' to this 'forbidden food'. After the feast they went to church to pray. Countries have <u>different</u> names for this day. 'Mardi Gras' means 'fat Tuesday' and the word 'carnival' means 'goodbye to meat'.

On Pancake Day in some places there are pancake <u>races</u>, <u>too</u>. The most famous race in England <u>takes place</u> at Olney in the <u>county</u> of Buckinghamshire. It starts at 11.55 a.m. and <u>contestants</u>, who are over 18 and live in Olney, wear a dress, an <u>apron</u> and a hat or a <u>scarf</u> and run from the <u>market square</u> to the church carrying a <u>frying pan</u>. In this pan there is a hot pancake. They <u>toss</u> this pancake at the beginning of the race and at the finish. The first person who runs the 415 yards (375 metres) is the <u>winner</u>. He or she then <u>serves</u> a pancake to the <u>bell ringer</u> and <u>gets a kiss</u> from him. The record time for the race is 63 seconds.

This pancake race began in 1445. A woman was in her kitchen and she <u>was cooking</u> pancakes. Suddenly she heard the church bell ringing. It was time to go to church. She <u>ran</u> out of her house to the church. She <u>was still carrying</u> her frying pan.

apron	Schürze	frying pan	Bratpfanne
bell ringer	Person, die die Glocken läutet	gets a kiss	bekommt einen Kuss
		Lent	Fastenzeit
was cooking	war gerade dabei zu kochen/backen	market square	Marktplatz
		pancakes	Pfannkuchen
was still carrying	trug immer noch	past	Vergangenheit
celebrations	Feierlichkeiten	race	Rennen
contestants	Konkurrenten	ran	lief
county	(in etwa) Landkreis, Grafschaft	scarf	Schal
		serves	serviert
different	andere	takes place	findet statt
fats	Fette	toss	hochwerfen und wieder fangen
feast	Festessen		
food	Essen, Lebensmittel	winner	Gewinner(in)
be forgiven	(Sünde) vergeben werden		

Reading for fun

6 The great British breakfast

Nowadays when everyone is very conscious of what they eat, not many families eat a traditional English breakfast. However, in British hotels, guest houses and Bed and Breakfast establishments the tradition is kept alive. A cup of coffee, one or two rolls and jam – what is called the continental breakfast – is definitely not a breakfast for the British on holiday.

So what IS? – Eggs of some sort: fried, poached or scrambled, two rashers of bacon, a grilled tomato, a short, fat sausage and maybe some mushrooms and baked beans. In Wales or Yorkshire you can add a slice of black pudding. In Scotland on a cold winter's morning you can order a bowl of porridge to start with and smoked fish is often on the breakfast menu, too. You then need to leave room for your toast and marmalade (jam made of citrus fruit) and finish with a pot of strong tea.

Hotels might be more expensive in Britain than in your home country, but for value for money there is nothing better than the good British breakfast.

add	dazugeben	mushrooms	Pilze
baked beans	gebackene Bohnen	nowadays	heutzutage
bowl	Schüssel	order	bestellen
black pudding	Blutwurst	poached eggs	pochierte Eier
definitely	bestimmt	pot	Kanne
establishments	Häuser	porridge	Haferbrei
fried	gebraten	rasher of bacon	Scheibe gebratener Speck
however	jedoch, aber	rolls	Brötchen/Semmel
jam	Marmelade	scrambled eggs	Rühreier
is kept alive	wird am Leben gehalten	slice	Scheibe
leave room for	Platz lassen für	smoked	geräuchert
marmalade	Orangenmarmelade	strong	stark
maybe	vielleicht	value for money	gutes Preis-/ Leistungsverhältnis
menu	Speisekarte		
might	(hier:) könnten		

Reading for fun

7 The holiday postcard

When young people go on holiday <u>nowadays</u> or when they travel round the world in their gap year – in the year after they finish their studies and before they start their first job – they often send e-mails and digital pictures to their families and friends. Many people, <u>however</u>, still send picture postcards.

On October 1st 1870 the UK Post Office produced the first official postcard with a <u>pre-printed</u> stamp on it. It cost a halfpenny and a stamp for a normal letter cost one penny. 675,000 people wanted to buy this new postcard on the first day and they waited patiently outside post offices. In some towns there were so many people that the police <u>supervised</u> them!

In 1894, the Post Office <u>introduced</u> special <u>adhesive</u> stamps for postcards, so that there could be the first photographic postcards. From this date postcards were cheaper to produce because there was no pre-printed stamp on them. The first known photographic card in the UK was a picture of Scarborough, a seaside town on the Yorkshire coast in the north-east of England.

One side of these cards was left <u>free</u> for the name and address and the stamp, so people wrote the <u>message</u> on the same side as the picture. In 1902, the UK was the first country that introduced the use of the <u>divided back</u>. On one side of the card there was a line that divided this side into two <u>halves</u>. So it was <u>possible</u> to have the message and the address on one side of the postcard and the picture on the other. This was the <u>beginning</u> of the picture postcard that we <u>know</u> today.

adhesive	haftend, klebend	know	kennen
beginning	Anfang	message	Mitteilung
divided back	geteilte Rückseite	nowadays	heutzutage
free	unbeschriftet, blanko	possible	möglich
one half, two halves	eine Hälfte, zwei Hälften	pre-printed	vorgedruckt
however	jedoch, aber	side	Seite
introduce	(hier) einführen	supervise	überwachen

Reading for fun

8 The Guinness book of records

You probably know the Guinness book of records where you can read about the richest dog in the world, the longest salami, the fastest window cleaner, the best British summer. But have you ever read about people who are famous for a very bad reason?

The most expensive taxi ride
The Leipzig book fair takes place once a year in, of course, Leipzig. Publishers meet to discuss books but also to have a lot of parties. One year at this event the French publishers Rémy Gautier left his fifth party in two hours and found a taxi. He gave the taxi driver a card with the name and address of his Leipzig hotel on it and then fell asleep on the back seat of the taxi. Next morning he woke up outside his home in Paris because he had shown the taxi driver the wrong card.

The worst cough
Bob Pople of Melbourne had the worst cough in recent history. He often got coughs and colds in the winter (in August in Australia!) so when he got a cough he went to bed early, but he still coughed and coughed and coughed all through the night. His neighbour woke up and thought the noise was from a gun. She called the police who answered her call very quickly. Armed policemen wearing protective clothing surrounded the house.
When everything was ready a police officer knocked on the door. He was very surprised when it opened and they saw a sleepy man with a red nose coughing into a large handkerchief. Mr Pople said he usually took cough medicine for his cough, but he didn't have any in the house and it was a Sunday. He promised to go to the doctor's the next morning to get some.

book fair	Buchmesse	promise	versprechen
cough	Husten; husten	protective clothing	Schutzkleidung
discuss	diskutieren	recent	(hier:) jüngste
fell asleep	schlief ein	surround	umringen
handkerchief	Taschentuch	takes place	findet statt
knock	klopfen		

Reading for fun

9 The Teddy bear

Have you still got your childhood teddy bear? Have you ever wondered why it is called 'teddy bear'?

The story began in Giengen in southern Germany in 1847 when Margarete Steiff was born. She loved sewing and she was the first person in Giengen who bought a sewing machine. With this she started her own dressmaking business and made dresses and coats. In 1879 she produced the first of the now famous stuffed animals, an elephant. More animals followed. In 1892 Margarete Steiff sold the first bears for children and from then on her business grew and grew. The big breakthrough came at the Leipzig toy fair of 1903 when a buyer from a New York toy company ordered 3,000 toys. After this the Steiff bear became a big hit in America.

President Theodor Roosevelt (his friends called him Teddy) often went hunting and one day he refused to shoot a bear cub during a four-day hunting trip in Mississippi. The next day Clifford Berryman drew the first cartoon with Roosevelt and a bear and after this there was always a bear in the cartoons he drew of Roosevelt. As a result the bear became known as Teddy's bear.

This was good news for Steiff and by 1907 the company had sold half a million bears. The teddy bear is still one of the most popular toys world-wide.

bear cub	*Bärenjunges*	*ordered*	*bestellte*
breakthrough	*Durchbruch*	*refused*	*weigerte sich*
childhood	*Kindheit*	*as a result*	*infolgedessen*
drew	*zeichnete*	*sewing*	*nähen*
during	*während*	*sewing machine*	*Nähmaschine*
fair	*Messe*	*shoot*	*schießen*
followed	*folgten*	*had sold*	*hatte verkauft*
grew	*wuchs*	*stuffed*	*ausgestopft*
went hunting	*ging auf die Jagd*	*toy*	*Spielzeug*
news	*Nachricht*	*wonder*	*sich fragen*

Reading for fun

10 Opening hours

There are a lot of things a visitor should know when you go to Britain and want to have a drink in a pub: Go up to the bar and order and pay for your drink before you sit down. Don't wait for someone to serve you! You can't pay for beer on a credit card. If you want to pay by credit card, order something to eat <u>as well</u> and then it is OK.

Traditionally, the <u>licensing laws</u> in Britain are stricter than in continental Europe. It all began in the 1660s. The government <u>needed</u> money so they <u>raised</u> <u>tax revenue</u> <u>by taxing</u> beer, coffee, chocolate and tea but there was no tax on gin or whisky. A lot of people got drunk so the government then introduced licences for places that wanted to sell these <u>spirits</u>. Much later in 1872 it became illegal to sell spirits to children under sixteen. The age was <u>even lower</u> in 1886 when <u>anyone</u> over 13 could drink in a pub. This sounds <u>strange</u> to us but remember that at that time a girl of 12 and a boy of 13 could get married legally! Of course, you have to be 18 now if you want to drink alcohol in a pub in Britain. You can have a drink with a meal in pubs when you are 16 but you have to be with an <u>adult</u>.

So you could drink in a pub that had a licence, but *when* could you have a drink? In 1921, nine hours drinking were allowed in London and eight hours in the rest of the country between 11 o'clock in the morning and 10 o'clock at night. Pubs had to close for two hours in the afternoon.
On Sundays pubs could stay open for five hours <u>except</u> in Wales and the county of Monmouthshire where pubs were closed. Sunday was a day to go to chapel and pray and not a day to go drinking.
<u>Gradually</u>, the hours for drinking got longer and longer but pubs <u>still</u> closed at 10.30 or 11 o'clock at night. The person at the bar called 'last orders, please' before closing time and then 'time gentlemen, please' ten minutes later. This ten-minute 'drinking-up time' started in 1961.

In 2004, the <u>government</u> of Britain introduced a new law that will <u>allow</u> some pubs and clubs to stay open for 24 hours a day from November 2005. Many people who want longer opening hours are very happy but some policemen are not because they think a lot of people will get very drunk just like in the 1660s!

adult	Erwachsene, r	*gradually*	allmählich
allow	erlauben	*licensing laws*	Schankgesetze
anyone	(hier) jeder	*need*	brauchen, nötig haben
as well	auch	*raised*	erhöhten, angehoben
by taxing	durch Besteuerung von	*spirits*	Spirituosen
even lower	noch niedriger	*still*	immer noch
except	außer	*strange*	seltsam
government	Regierung	*tax revenue*	Steuereinnahmen

Reading for fun

11 Celebrations

On the last Thursday in November the American people celebrate Thanksgiving. It is a time for families to meet and is one of the most important celebrations of the year. The word itself tells us that it is a time when people 'give thanks' for a good harvest. The first Thanksgiving was in 1621 when the Pilgrim fathers, who had sailed from England to start a new life in America, had an autumn harvest feast with the Wampanoag Indians.

On 25th December people in Britain celebrate Christmas – the name means the birth of Christ. Children open their presents on this day and not on Christmas Eve, the 24th December. The 26th December in Britain is called Boxing Day. It has nothing to do with the sport of boxing. The day after Christmas was the day when servants from the big houses had a day off and their employers gave them their Christmas presents or Christmas boxes. Most people still give the postman, the paper boy or girl, the milkman or milklady, the refuse collectors a tip at Christmas, though maybe not on Boxing Day.

Turkey is often on the menu for these two great celebrations. In America, the turkey for Thanksgiving is stuffed with corn bread or chestnuts and served with mashed potatoes, cranberry sauce, baked carrots and Brussels sprouts. In Britain, it is stuffed with sage and onion or with sausage meat and it is served with roast potatoes and Brussels sprouts and sometimes sausages, too.

Pumpkin pie or pecan pie is often in the Thanksgiving dinner menu. You see pumpkins in America from Halloween onwards until Thanksgiving. At Halloween children sometimes hollow out a pumpkin, put a candle inside it and use it as a lantern when they go from house to house and knock on doors saying:

"Trick or treat. Give me some sweets. If you don't you will regret it!"

In most houses in Britain Christmas dinner finishes with Christmas pudding or plum pudding. The name is very confusing. It doesn't have plums in it! Before the mixture is steamed the cook hangs it in a cloth bag in a warm place and it slowly gets bigger and fills the bag. When the pudding has filled the bag – when the pudding is 'plum' – you can cook it. It is good luck for everyone to help stir the Christmas pudding. A long time ago the person who made the Christmas pudding put silver sixpences into it. You can, of course, still put money in the pudding today, but the money isn't made of silver!

birth	Geburt	it has nothing to do with	es hat nichts mit ... zu tun
Brussels sprouts	Rosenkohl	plums	Pflaumen
candle	Kerze	pumpkin	Kürbis
chestnuts	süsse Kastanien	refuse collector	Müllwerker
confusing	verwirrend	regret it	es bereuen
cranberry sauce	Soße aus Preiselbeeren	sage	Salbei
a day off	ein freier Tag	sailed from	mit dem Schiff weggefahren
employers	Arbeitgeber	sausage meat	Füllung aus Würstchen
feast	Festessen	servants	Bedienstete
fill	füllen	sixpence	ein altes Geldstück
harvest	Ernte	steamed	gedünstet
hollow out	aushöhlen	stir	umrühren
itself	selbst	stuffed	gefüllt
knock	klopfen	a tip	Trinkgeld
lantern	Laterne		
mashed potatoes	Kartoffelbrei		

Reading for fun

12 Have a holiday in a historic building

"We stayed for a long weekend in Robin Hood's Hut – the view of the Welsh mountains was wonderful." "We spent two weeks in The Ruin – the famous architect Robert Adam worked on the building." "Bob and Barbara had a holiday in Freston Tower overlooking the estuary of the river Orwell."
Do these remarks sound more interesting to you than "I stayed in the Central Hotel"? If the answer is "yes", then maybe you will be interested in the charity The Landmark Trust.

It is a British charity that Sir John and Lady Smith founded in 1965 and its aim is to restore interesting historic buildings. Restoration work is expensive so when it is finished The Landmark Trust lets the buildings for holidays. The Trust's motto is: 'Ensure our past has a future.' What will your holiday be like if you book with The Landmark Trust? Some of the landmarks are small, only big enough for two people, some are very big and 12 or more people can sleep in them. Some are in open countryside or in a large park or garden, others are in the middle of a city. All of them are special in some way, because of where they are, because of their history, or because of the person who built them. When The Landmark Trust works on old buildings they prefer to mend rather than renew so that these buildings keep some of their original character.

If you pay for a holiday in one of these buildings, you will be the owner of it for a short time. You can enjoy and use all of it, cook, sleep and play in it. The Trust provides guests with books and a photo album in each landmark so you will learn about the history of the building and why and how the builders made it as they did. You will enjoy learning about the history of the building but you won't live as the people did when it was first built – there are modern bathrooms and heating in all the properties. The Trust provides you with towels and the kitchens are well-equipped. The bigger properties have dishwashers, freezers and washing machines, but you won't find televisions or microwaves in any of these properties.

There are always new buildings that need restoring. The Trust is going to help with the restoration of Queen Anne's Summer House in Bedfordshire*, Glenmalloch Lodge in Dumfries & Galloway* in Scotland and the Warder's Tower in Staffordshire*.
If you want to see pictures of these future landmarks then visit the web-site at www.landmarktrust.org.uk

* Grafschaften in Großbritanien

aim	Ziel	overlooking	mit Blick auf
charity	Wohltätigkeitsorganisation	prefer	vorziehen
countryside	auf dem Land; Landschaft	provides	bereitstellen, zur Verfügung stellen
estuary	Mündung		
ensure	sicher stellen	properties	Immobilien
found	gründen	renew	erneuern
future	Zukunft, zukünftig	towels	Handtücher
keep	behalten	tower	Turm
let	vermieten	view	Aussicht
mend	reparieren	well-equipped	gut ausgestattet
owner	Besitzer		